His Name is One

~~~~~~~~~~~~~~~~~~~~~~~~

An Hebraic look at the ancient Hebrew meanings of the names of God

Jeff A. Benner
~~~~~~~~~~~~~~~~~~~~~~~~

His Name is One

Unless otherwise noted, scripture passages are translated by the author.

When noted as KJV, the scriptures are taken from the KING JAMES BIBLE.

Ancient Hebrew Research Center
P.O. Box 12675 Reading, Pa 19612

"His Name is One," by Jeff A. Benner. ISBN 1-58939-457-7.

Published 2003 by Virtualbookworm.com Publishing Inc., P.O. Box 9949, College Station, TX, 77842, US.

Manufactured in the United States of America.

To my children, Kristina, Dallas, Josiah, Jeremiah and Jedidiah.

Table of Contents

Introduction 1

Chapter 1 - Name 4

Chapter 2 - One 19

Chapter 3 - His name is One 24

Chapter 4 - Spirit 28

Chapter 5 - God 32

Chapter 6 - El Shaddai 43

Chapter 7 - Yahweh 49

Chapter 8 - Lord 61

Chapter 9 - Angel 67

Chapter 10 - King 74

Chapter 11 - Father 80

Chapter 12 - Savior 89

Chapter 13 - Shepherd 97

Chapter 14 - Creator 103

Chapter 15 - Jealous......106

Chapter 16 - Everlasting......109

Chapter 17 - Holy......110

Conclusion......112

Appendix A......116

Bibliography......119

Introduction

The purpose of this book is to uncover the original Hebraic meanings of the various names of God that flow out of the ancient Hebrew language of the Bible. The ancient authors of the Bible were Hebrews who lived in an Eastern Oriental culture. In order to interpret their writings appropriately, they must be understood through their culture rather than our Western Greco-Roman culture. The modern translations, dictionaries and commentaries of the Biblical texts have interpreted the Bible through a Western perspective often ignoring the culture, in which the texts were originally written.

The title of this book, "His name is One," is from Zechariah 14:9 and was chosen because of the passages unique ability to express the full character of God. A verse such as this has very little meaning in our modern Western culture, but, when understood in its original Eastern culture, it beautifully expresses the nature of God. By placing the names of God, and other Hebrew words, back into the Hebrew culture and their original context, the words and passages begin to take on a shape often hidden to the average reader of the Bible.

Eastern and Western Culture

In the world, past and present, there are two major types of cultures, Eastern and Western. The ancient Hebrews and other ancient Semitic cultures as well as today's Orientals of the Far East, and the Bedouins of the Near and Middle East, see the world through Eastern cultural eyes.

The ancient Greeks and Romans as well as today's European and American cultures see the world through Western cultural eyes. The modern Hebrews are mostly comprised of transplanted Europeans and also belong to the Western culture.

These Eastern and Western cultures view their surroundings, lives, and purpose in ways that would seem foreign to the other. Through this book we will be looking at a few of the differences between these two cultures. To more fully understand the ancient texts of the Bible, which were written in the ancient Eastern culture of the Hebrews, we must place ourselves within their culture rather than reading the text through the eyes of the modern Western culture.

Biblical Interpretation

When you pick up your Bible to read it, two forms of Biblical interpretation are at work at the same time. The first is the translator's interpretation of what the original Hebrew text means. The translator decides how the text should be translated into a modern Western language for the average modern reader. The second is the English readers' interpretation of what the English translation means. The interpretation of the translator will have a direct influence on the outcome of the English readers' interpretation and the reader's culture will influence how he reads the translation.

As we examine the various Hebrew names of God, we must always keep in mind that the ancient Hebrew culture and language, in which the ancient Biblical text was written is very different from our own English culture and language. One of the most common mistakes in Biblical interpretation is to allow our own cultural and linguistic characteristics to be interjected into the interpretation of the text.

In order to fully comprehend the original writers' understanding of the texts he created, we must immerse ourselves in his culture and language, training our minds to read the texts through his eyes and mind.

Chapter 1 - Name

Your *name* O LORD is forever, your fame O LORD is for generation after generation.
Psalms 135:13

Biblical Names

In our modern culture a name is nothing more than an identifier, usually chosen by our parents because they like the sound of the name or it is the name of a favorite relative or ancestor. This is not true of the ancient cultures, such as the Hebrews, where a name was a representation of whom the individual was, based on his character and function.

One of the major differences between our Western culture and the Eastern culture of the ancient Hebrews is how someone or something is described. The Hebrew was not so concerned with the appearance of someone or something, as he was with its function. A Western mind would describe a common pencil according to its appearance, something like; "it is yellow and about eight inches long." An Eastern mind describes the same pencil according to its function, something like; "I write and erase words with it." Notice that the Eastern description uses the verbs "write" and "erase," while the Western description uses the adjectives "yellow" and "long." Because of Hebrew's form of functional descriptions, verbs are used much more frequently then adjectives in the Bible.

A good example of the Hebrew language's functional descriptions can be found in the word "איל" (ayil). This word, depending on the translation, is shown as an oak tree, ram, mighty *men* or a post as can be seen in the following verses from the King James Version.

> "And Abraham lifted up his eyes, and looked, and behold behind him a ram caught in a thicket by his horns: and Abraham went and took the ram, and offered him up for a burnt offering in the stead of his son."
> Genesis 22:13 (KJV)

> "He made also posts of three-score cubits, even unto the post of the court round about the gate."
> Ezekiel 40:14 (KJV)

> "For they shall be ashamed of the oaks which ye have desired, and ye shall be confounded for the gardens that ye have chosen."
> Isaiah 1:29 (KJV)

> "Then the dukes of Edom shall be amazed; the mighty men of Moab, trembling shall take hold upon them; all the inhabitants of Canaan shall melt away."
> Exodus 15:15 (KJV)

The original meaning of the word "איל" (ayil) is a "strong leader." An oak tree is the hardest and strongest of the woods in the forest, the ram is the strong leader among the flock. A post is the strong upright pillar that supports the structure. The mighty men are the strong leaders of the community. The translators have taken the above passages, originally written from an Eastern perspective, and altered the original meaning in order for the text to make sense to a Western reader. Because of the many different ways the Eastern texts can be translated, differences in translations often occur. Psalms 29:9 includes the Hebrew word "אילה" (ayalah), the feminine form of "איל" (ayil), and is translated two different ways in two common translations.

> "The voice of the LORD makes the deer to calve." (NASB)

> "The voice of the LORD twists the oaks." (NIV)

While our Western mind sees no similarity between a deer and an oak, and would never describe them in the same way, the Hebrew's Eastern mind sees them as identical, both being functionally the same as "strong leaders." A more literal rendering of this verse in Hebrew thought would be:

> "The voice of the LORD makes the <u>strong leaders</u> twist."

When reading the Bible, the reader will become more aware of the meaning of a text if he remembers to look for the function of a particular object or the role of an individual, rather than its appearance. To illustrate this important aspect, let us look at the "ark" of Noah and its description as found in Genesis 6:15.

> "And this is how you are to make the ark, three hundred cubits long, fifty cubits wide and thirty cubits high."

Our Western mind immediately begins to paint a picture of what the ark looks like based on the dimensions provided in the passage. If this was the author's intention, he did a poor job, as the description provided simply describes a long box and does not inform the reader of what the ark "looks" like. When we remember that the Hebrew author is attempting to describe the "function" of the ark we find that he is informing the reader of its immense size, as the "function" of the ark is to hold a very large number of animals.

Hebrew names have meanings that are lost when translated into English. The Hebrew word "אדם" (adam) means "man" and is also the name of the first man, Adam.

> "The LORD God formed the man (אדם) from the dust of the ground."
> Genesis 2.7

English translations completely erase the Hebraic connection between the "man" and his origin. When we place the original Hebrew words back into the text, we can see the connection between the words in the verse.

> "And the LORD formed the adam from the dust of adamah (ground)."

Below are a few other examples of the relationship between an individual's name and his function or role.

> "And she bore Cain and she said I have cain (acquired) a man."
> Genesis 4:1

> "And she bore a son and called his name Seth because God seth (placed) a seed to replace Abel."
> Genesis 4:25

> "And he called his name Noah saying he will noah (comfort) us."
> Genesis 5:29

> "And to Eber were born two sons, the name of one is Peleg because in his days the land was peleg (divided)."
> Genesis 10.25

Because Bible translations transliterate a name, such as "נח" into "Noah" and translate, into English, the same word "נח" into "comfort," the translation converts the meaning and essence of the name into simple "identifiers." As we shall see through this book, the nature and character of God is found within his names, which are lost in our translations and Western view of scripture.

Just as a name can give us a clue about the individual's character, we can also find some interesting clues about the character of the family lineage. Below is a list of the sons of Adam, the lineage of the promised Messiah, as found in Genesis chapter 5 with the Hebraic meaning for each name:

Adam	man
Seth	appoint (set in place)
Enosh	mortal (also means man, as man is mortal)
Kenan	dwelling place (literally a nest)
Mahalalel	light of God (also mcans praise as it illuminates another.)
Jared	comes down
Enoch	dedicate
Methuselah	his death brings
Lamech	despair
Noah	comfort

When the meanings of these names are combined, we discover a very interesting prophecy of the coming Messiah based on the functional descriptions of the names of Adam's descendents.

> "Man appointed a mortal dwelling, the light of God will come down dedicated, his death brings the despairing comfort."

Root System of Words

The word "name" is the usual translation for the Hebrew word "שם" (shem). Though the word "shem" has the meaning of a "name," the Hebraic meaning of the word goes far beyond our simple Western understanding of a "name." Depending on the translation, this Hebrew word is also translated as; fame, famous, honor, renown or report. Obviously, this Hebrew word has a broader meaning in the ancient Hebrew language. In order to discover its true meaning, we need to understand how the Hebrew language works. Hebrew words are built using a system of roots based on the twenty-two letters of the Hebrew alphabet, which form the foundation to the language. A chart of the Hebrew alphabet can be seen in appendix A.

When two of these letters are combined, a two letter "parent root" is formed. These parent roots are the most ancient Hebrew words and are usually words that are absolutely necessary for any communication to occur. Below are a few examples of these two letter parent roots.

אב (abh)	father	חם (hham)	cheese
אח (ahh)	brother	כן (ken)	yes
אל (el)	god	לא (lo)	no
אם (em)	mother	לב (lebh)	heart
אש (esh)	fire	מד (mad)	garment
בן (ben)	son	מר (mar)	bitter
בר (bar)	clean	קב (qabh)	jar
הר (har)	hill	שם (shem)	name

These parent roots are often expanded into a three consonant root by doubling the last letter of the root but will retain the same meaning as the original two-letter root.

בר (clean) to ברר (clean)

הר (hill) to הרר (hill)
לב (heart) to לבב (heart)
מד (garment) to מדד (garment)
מר (bitter) to מרר (bitter)
קב (jar) to קבב (jar)

Child roots are formed by attaching an “א,””ה,””ו” or “י” to the parent root. The modern Hebrew language recognizes these four letters as consonants, but in ancient times they also doubled as vowels. Each child root formed will be directly related in meaning to the original parent root. Below are the child roots, and their meanings formed from the parent root “בל (bal)” meaning “flow.”

אבל wilt: flowing away of life
הבל empty: flowing out of contents
בהל panic: flowing of the insides
בלה aged: flowing away of youth
בול flood: flowing of water
יבל stream: flowing of water

While the parent and child roots are most probably the original language of the Hebrews, other roots were adopted into the language over time out of the original roots. The most common adopted roots were formed by adding the letter “נ” (n) to the parent root. Adopted roots such as, “נאף” (na’aph), meaning adultery and “אנף” (anaph), meaning anger, are derived from the parent root “אף” (aph), which can mean nose, anger or passion. While it seems strange to us that the same Hebrew word is used for a nose as well as anger and passion, the Hebrews saw anger and passion as acts which cause heavy breathing resulting in the flaring of the nostrils, or nose.

Words are formed out of the parent and child roots by placing specific letters within the root. Some of the most common letter additions are an "מ" (m) or "ת" (t) in front or behind the original root, an "ה" (h), "ון" (on) or "ות"(ut) behind the root, or a "י" (y) or "ו" (o) in the middle of the root. These words are always related in meaning to the original root, out of which they came.

Now that we have a basic understanding of how the Hebrew root system of words work, let us examine the roots and words which are derived from the parent root "שם" (shem - name), all of which will aid with the finding of the original Hebraic meaning of the word.

Breath

The Hebrew word "נשמה" (neshemah) is formed by adding the letter "ה" (h) to the adopted root "נשם" (nasham) which comes from the parent root "שם" (shem). This word is used in Genesis 2:7 and means "breath."

> "And the LORD God formed the man of dust from the ground and he blew in his nostrils the breath (נשמה) of life and the man became a living soul."

While the Western mind simply sees "breath" as the exchange of air within the lungs, the ancient Hebrew mind understood the "breath" in an entirely different way as can be seen in Job 32:8:

> "The wind within man and the breath (נשמה) of the Almighty teach them."

Our Western understanding of the breath does not easily grasp the concept that a breath can teach. While our Western understanding can easily associate thoughts and emotions as the function of the "mind," the Easterner sees the same function in the "breath." The "breath" of both men and God has the ability to carry thought and emotion.

Skies

The next word that we will examine is the child root "שמה" (shamah) meaning "heaven," "sky" or "the place of the winds." It is always used in the plural form "שמים" (shamayim).

> "In the beginning God created the skies (שמים) and the land."
> Genesis 1:1

The Hebrew mind sees "נשמה" (neshemah) and "שמה" (shamah) as synonyms. The "נשמה" is the breath/wind of a man, and the "שמה" is the breath/wind of the skies. Just as we saw above where the נשמה can teach, so also the שמים (shamayim) can also speak.

> "The skies (שמים) proclaim his righteousness, and all the people see his glory."
> Psalms 97:6

Dry Wind

The root word "שמם" (shamam) is formed by doubling the second letter of the parent root. By adding the letter "ה"

(h) to the end, the word "שממה" (shememah) is formed. Both words mean, "desolate" and are used in the following passage.

> "Many shepherds will ruin my vineyards, they will trample my fields, they will turn the fields of my delight into a desert of desolation (שממה). And it will be made into desolation (שממה), parched and desolate (שמם) before me, all the land will be desolate (שמם) because there is no man to care for it."
> Jeremiah 12:10,11

When the dry winds blow through the desert, any moisture in the ground or air is removed causing the desert to become dry and parched. "שמם" (shamam) and "שממה" (shememah) are dry and desolate places formed by a dry wind.

Another child root "ישם" (yasham), with the same meaning as "שמם" (shamam), a dry desolating wind, can be seen in the following verse.

> "All your resting places of the cities will become dry, and the high places will be desolate (ישם)."
> Ezekiel 6:6

Shem

By gathering together all the words derived from the parent root "שם" (shem), and looking for the common thread that each have in common, we can discover the original Hebraic meaning of the parent root. Each of the words has the basic meaning of a "wind" within them. "נשמה" (neshemah) is the wind, or breath, of man, "שמים" (shamayim) is the wind of the skies, "שמם" (shamam), "שממה" (shememah) and "ישם" (yasham) is the desolation caused by a dry wind. From this we can conclude that the ancient Hebraic meaning of "שם" is "wind" or "breath."

The "שם" of a man is his breath, which in the Hebraic Eastern mind is the essence or character of the individual. The actions of the individual will always be related to his character. From this we understand that the "שם," the breath, is the place of origin of all the actions of the individual. The following are a few passages that demonstrate this Hebraic understanding of "שם."

> "O God, in your <u>name</u> (שם) save me; and in your strength rescue me."
> Psalms 54:1

A very common form of Hebrew poetry is called parallelism, where one idea is stated in two different ways. By studying these forms of poetry we can see into the Hebrew mind by observing how he paralleled one word with another. In the verse above, the phrase "in your name save me," is paralleled with the phrase "in your strength rescue me." From this passage we see that the Hebrews equated one's "name" with his "strength," an attribute of character.

> "O LORD, your <u>name</u> (שם) is forever; O LORD, your fame is from generation to generation."
> Psalms 135:13

In this passage, שם is paralleled with "fame." The Hebrew word for "fame" is "זכר" (zakar) which literally means "remembrance." The "fame" of the LORD are his "actions" that will be remembered throughout the generations. Through the poetic imagery of this verse, we see that the psalmist equated the "שם" of the LORD with his actions.

> "I will declare your [the LORD's] name (שם) to my brothers; within the assembly I will praise you."
> Psalms 22.22

In this passage, the phrase "I will declare your name" is parallel with "I will praise you," paralleling the שם (shem) of the LORD with "you," the LORD himself.

> "Your [David's] God will make the name (שם) of Solomon more beautiful than your name (שם) and his throne greater than your throne."
> 1 Kings 1.47

The poetry of this passage parallels the name of Solomon with his throne, a difficult concept for a Western thinker to grasp. Let us remember that the throne is not to be thought of in terms of physical description, but in function. The function of the throne is "authority," a characteristic of the king. The "שם" of Solomon is his "authority."

Names and Titles

A common mistake in Biblical interpretation is to make a distinction between a name and a title. For example, "King David," is often understood as containing the "name" "David" (an identifier) and his "title" "King." The Hebrew word דוד (david) literally means; "beloved," or "one who loves" and is descriptive of David's character. The Hebrew word מלך (melek) literally means "ruler" or "one who rules," also descriptive of David's character. As we can see, both of these words are descriptive of David's character. The Hebrews made no such distinction between a name and a title. The phrase "King David" is Hebraicly understood as "the one who *rules* is the one who *loves,*" a very fitting title for the great benevolent king of Israel and the friend of God.

Prayer

Because of the misunderstanding of the use of the word "name," some passages have been misinterpreted causing a belief that was not originally intended by the author. For instance, it is a common practice to conclude each prayer with the phrase, "In the name of Jesus, Amen." This custom is based on the following passages.

> "And I will do whatever you ask in my name, so that the Son may bring glory to the Father."
> John 14:13 (NIV)

> "I tell you the truth, my Father will give you whatever you ask in my name."
> John 16:23 (NIV)

Are the passages above informing us that in order for a prayer to be heard we must use the "formula," "in the name of Jesus"? What is the purpose of this "formula"? This phrase was not meant to be a "formula" attached to the end of each prayer, but the spirit in which the prayer is given. According to the Hebraic understanding of the word "name" we can translate these passages using the word "character" rather than "name." What Jesus is telling us is that when we pray we should pray in his character. Our prayers should be given in the same spirit, conviction, faith and purpose that his prayers would be given.

Chapter 2 - One

Listen Israel, Yahweh is our God,
Yahweh is *One*
Deuteronomy 6:4

Just as the Hebraism of the word "שם" (shem) is lost through its translation into the English word "name," the Hebraism of the word "אחד" (ehhad) is lost through its translation into the English word "one." By examining the parent and child roots related to "אחד," we can again find the Hebraic meaning of this word just as we did with the word "שם."

Hhad

The child root "אחד" (ehhad) is derived from the parent root "חד" (hhad). Up to this point we have seen the Hebrew words written with the "modern" Hebrew alphabet (see appendix A). The ancient Hebrew alphabet was originally written with pictographs (meaning picture writing) similar to Egyptian hieroglyphs (see appendix A). Over the centuries, these ancient pictographic letters evolved into the Modern Hebrew alphabet.

These original pictographs supplied meaning to the word. As an example the Hebrew word for "son" is "בן" (ben) and is written as "𐤍𐤁" in the original pictographic script. The first letter is "𐤁" (b). This is a picture of the floor plan of a common nomadic tent as would have been used by Abraham. The tent is divided into two parts, one side for the males of the household and the other for the females. A wall separates the two sides with an opening in the back allowing for passage between the two sides. The entrance into the tent is on the male side, as seen at the top left of the pictograph. The meaning of this letter is tent, house and family.

The second letter, "𐤍" (n) is a picture of a germinating seed. A seed is the offspring of the previous generation, which grows producing seeds for the next generation. This concept of perpetuity, or continuance is the meaning of this letter.

When these two letters are combined the parent root "𐤁𐤍" (ben) is formed, with the original Hebraic meaning being "the house that continues." The function of a "son" is to continue the family line to the next generation.

The Hebrew parent root word "חד" (hhad) is written as "𐤇𐤃" in the ancient Hebrew pictographs. The first letter in this word is "𐤇" (hh), representing a tent wall, such as that which divides the male from the female sides, and means to separate or divide. The second letter, "𐤃" (d), represents a door or entrance, such as that which allows passage between the two sides of the tent, and means to enter. Our parent root "𐤇𐤃" (hhad) has the pictographic meaning of "a wall with a door" or "a wall for entering." The Hebraic idea being expressed in this word is that one thing, or person, serves more than one function. Just as the wall separates the two sides, the door in the wall unites them. This Hebraic imagery can be clearly seen in the following passage:

> "And you son of man, the sons of your people are speaking about you next to the *walls* and in the *doors* of the houses; and <u>one</u> (חד) speaks at <u>one</u> (אחד) man and at his brother saying please come and hear what the word of the one coming from the LORD is saying. And they come to you like they are coming of a people, and my people sit before you. And they listen to your words but they do not practice it; adoration is in their mouths but their hearts walk after their greed."
> Ezekiel 33:30,31.

In this passage we see the two opposite actions of the people. While they go to hear from the LORD, they practice evil in their hearts, "one" individual with two opposite manifestations. It is also interesting to note that Ezckicl shows that these people are speaking about him at the walls and doors, a direct connection to the word "חד/," whose pictographs are of a wall and a door.

Riddle

The child root "חוד" (hhud), derived from the parent root "חד" (hhad), has the meaning of a riddle.

> "Son of man, give a riddle (חוד) of a riddle (חידה - hhiydah, feminine form of hhud); and give a parable of a parable to the house of Israel."
> Ezekiel 17:2

From the Hebrew poetry of this verse we can see that the word חוד (hhud) is similar to a parable. A riddle or parable presents a story to an audience, using events and people familiar to the listeners. Then, the one giving the parable presents a twist that cannot be understood easily. Keeping in mind the pictographs of the word "חד" (hhad), this "twist" in the story is the wall that separates the listener from the meaning of the parable. When the speaker explains the parable, the door is opened and the listeners are united with the meaning.

> "The kingdom of heaven is like treasure hidden in a field. When a man found it, he hid it again, and then in his joy went and sold all he had and bought that field."
> Matthew 13:44

Jesus used this form of teaching frequently as in the example above. While the idea of selling all possessions in order to buy a field with an even larger value due to the treasure, is easily understood, its connection to the kingdom of heaven is a bit more mysterious. Those who understood the teachings of Jesus easily understand that the kingdom of heaven is of greater value than any worldly possessions and these people are united with Jesus in its meanings, while those who do not understand the meaning are separated. When asked why he spoke in parables, he said;

> "The knowledge of the secrets of the kingdom of heaven has been given to you, but not to them."
> Matthew 13:10

Unity

Another child root derived from the parent “חד” (hhad) is “אחד” (ehhad). The word “אחד,” keeping with our foundational meaning in the parent root, means those that are separated come together in unity. While this word is often translated as “one,” where the actual Hebraism is lost, it is better translated as a “unity.”

The Western mind sees “one” as a singular, void of any connection to something else. For instance, “one” man is an individual entity to himself, just as “one” tree is an entity to itself. To the ancient Hebrew Eastern mind, nothing is “one”; all things are dependent upon something else. A man is not “one,” but a unity of body, mind and breath that is expressed in the Hebrew word “נפש” (nephesh). The man is also in unity with his wife and family as well as with the larger community. Even a tree is a unity of roots, trunk, branches and leaves, which is also in unity with the surrounding landscape. “One” year is a unity of seasons. The first use of “אחד” (ehhad) is found in Genesis 1:5 where “evening” and morning,” two states of opposite function, are united to form “one” day.

> “And there was evening and there was morning, one day”

Chapter 3 - His name is One

Yahweh will be king over all the land, in that day the Yahweh will be one and *his name is One*
Zechariah 14:9

When we read that God is one, we quickly assume that this is relating to a number of one, because of our Western understanding of the word "one." We ignore the Hebraic understanding of the word "אחד" which identifies God as a unity within himself. The above passage is not attempting to place God within a box, which contains only one object, but an infinite God that can manifest in many ways, all of which are in unity. What does the idea of unity within God mean? In the book of Exodus, God reveals himself to Israel as two pillars.

> "And the LORD walked before them by day in a <u>pillar of cloud</u> to comfort them on the path and by night a <u>pillar of fire</u> to give light to them for walking by day and night."
> (Exodus 13:21)

Each of these manifestations of God, the pillar of cloud and the pillar of fire, is unique in its function. The pillar of fire provides heat during the cold nights as well as light in the darkness. The pillar of cloud provides shade from the heat of the sun. While the function of each pillar is distinct and separate from the other, they are also united in their functions in that both bring comfort to the people. The two clouds are "אחד" (ehhad), two separate actions with a common function.

God is not just a God of love, but a God of hate as well (Malachi 1:2,3). He is a God of mercy and justice. He is also a God of war and peace. He creates light and darkness, good and evil (Isaiah 45:7). Throughout the scriptures we see God raising up nations and tearing down nations all for the purpose of bringing about his will. While God manifests himself within two extremes, they are always in balance and in unity. The writer of Ecclesiastes best expresses this balance of unity. Just as God manifests these characteristics, his people who know the heart and will of God and his balance in unity, know the proper time and season for each of these characteristics to be applied.

> "There is a time for everything, and a season for every activity under heaven:
> A time to be born and a time to die,
> A time to plant and a time to uproot,
> A time to kill and a time to heal,
> A time to tear down and a time to build,
> A time to weep and a time to laugh,
> A time to morn and a time to dance,
> A time to scatter stones and a time to gather them,
> A time to embrace and time to refrain,
> A time to search and a time to give up,
> A time to keep and a time to throw away,
> A time to tear and time to mend,
> A time to be silent and a time to speak,

> A time to love and a time to hate,
> A time for war and a time for peace.
> Ecclesiastes 3:1-8

Now that we have a Hebraic understanding of the two key words in the title of this book, we can read the phrase through the eyes of the ancient Hebrew Zechariah who wrote it.

> "The LORD will be king over all the land,
> in that day the LORD will be one and <u>his name is one</u>."
> Zechariah 14:9

The final phrase of this verse in Hebrew is "שמו אחד" (sh'mo ehhad). Translators have interpreted this phrase several different ways, including:

> "his name the only name" (NIV)

> "his name the only one" (NASB)

> "his name one" (KJV)

All of these are the translators' attempts to make sense of the Hebrew phrase to an English reader. As we have discovered, the Hebrew word "שם" (shem) of God is the attributes of his character which is identified as "אחד" (ehhad), a unity. A translation reflecting the Hebraic understanding of this passage would be:

> "His character is in unity."

Or;

"His attributes and being, work together in unity."

God manifests himself in many different ways and for many different reasons. All of the names of God found in the Bible are a reflection of these manifestations of his character, all of which are in unity, revealing the nature of God. Let us now look at some of these names of God through the mind of the Biblical author rather than our Western minds.

Chapter 4 - Spirit

"and the *Spirit* of God hovered over the face of the waters."
Genesis 1:2

We have previously examined the Hebrew word "נשמה" (neshemah) meaning, breath or wind. Synonymous with "neshemah" is the Hebrew word "רוח" (ruahh), translated as "spirit" in the above passage. The following verses show, through parallelism, the similarity in meaning to both "נשמה" and "רוח."

> All the while my breath (neshemah) is in me and the wind (ruahh) of God is in my nose.
> Job 27:3

> The wind (ruahh) of God has made me and the breath (neshemah) of the Almighty has given me life.
> Job 33:4

While "רוח" means "breath" or "wind," the Hebraic meaning of this word has a unique meaning separate from "נשמה." Let us take a closer look at the word "רוח" by examining other root words that are also derived from the same parent root "רח" (RHh).

And from the excellent produce of the sun and from the excellent yield of the moon (ירח - yere'ahh).
Deuteronomy 33:14

A stranger did not lodge outside, I opened my door to the traveler (ארח - orehh) .
Job 31:32

All the firstborn in the land of Egypt will die, from the firstborn of Pharoah sitting on the throne to the firstborn of the maidservant who is behind the millstones (רחה - rehhah), and all the firstborn of the livestock.
Exodus 11:5

A millstone is a circular stone, about one foot in diameter. It is flat on the top and bottom and is a few inches thick. This stone has a hole bored through the middle from top to bottom. This stone is then set on top of another flat stone. The grain is poured through the hole and the millstone is turned around causing the grain between the two stones to be crushed and ground into meal.

All four of these words, "רוח" (ruahh - wind), "ירח" (yere'ahh - moon), "ארח" (orehh - traveler) and "רחה" (rehhah - millstone), have one thing in common, they all follow a prescribed path. The winds follow specific paths each season, the moon follows a prescribed path in the night sky, a traveler follows a prescribed path to his destination and a millstone follows a continual path with each revolution.

The "רוח" (ruahh - wind) cannot be seen, but the effects of the wind can. We can see the leaves of the tree moving in the wind and we can feel it against our bodies. In the same manner, God cannot be seen but we can see his effects all around us in his creation. Just as the winds follow a prescribed path through the seasons, God also follows a prescribed path; he is the same yesterday, today and forever.

God reveals himself to man by his character, which remains constant, his road is straight and he does not stray from this road. The Hebrew word for straight is "צדיק" (tsadiyq) and is often translated as "righteous." He also expects his children to follow on this same straight path.

The Road

> For the LORD knows the road of the righteous and the road of the wicked will perish.
> Psalm 1:6

> O, LORD, point me to your road and lead me on a level path.
> Psalm 27:11

Our life is a journey along the road that will lead to righteousness or wickedness. Just as the wind, or breath of the sky follows a prescribed path, our breath follows a prescribed path. When God gives us a new breath, his breath, he will cause us to follow his path.

> And I will give to them a new heart and a new breath I will give within them, and I will remove the heart of stone

> from their flesh and I will give to them a heart of flesh, and I will give within them my breath and I will cause them to do my statutes they are to walk and my laws they will guard and do them.
> Ezekiel 36:26,27

Only by receiving the breath of God can we follow the correct path.

Chapter 5 - God

"In the beginning *God* created the heavens and the earth."
Genesis 1:1

Let us begin our investigations of the names of God with the name by which he is most commonly called, "God." When you hear the word "God," what comes to mind? Our culture has produced two different views of who or what God is. The first is an old man with white hair and beard sitting in the clouds. While this seems more like a children's picture of God, it is many adults as well, probably because of the stories we hear as children, which remain with us into adulthood. Another common view is an invisible force that spans the universe, unknowable and untouchable. However we view God when reading the text, it is irrelevant, as we must learn to view God in the same manner that the ancient Hebrews who wrote the Biblical text did.

There are three different words used in the Bible that are translated as God; אל (el), אלה (eloah) and אלהים (elohiym). The first of these is a two-letter parent root and is the foundation for the other two that are derived from it.

Abstract vs. concrete thought

We have previously discussed the differences between the modern Western thinkers method of describing something compared to the ancient Hebrew Eastern thinker. Here we will look at another major difference between the two which impacts how we read the Biblical text.

The Eastern mind views the world through concrete thought that is expressed in ways that can be seen, touched, smelled, tasted or heard. An example of this can be found in Psalms 1:3 where the author expresses his thoughts in such concrete terms as; tree, streams of water, fruit, leaf and wither.

> "He is like a tree planted by streams of water, which yields its fruit in season, and whose leaf does not wither." (NIV)

The Western mind views the world through abstract thought that is expressed in ways that cannot be seen, touched, smelled, tasted or heard. Examples of Abstract thought can be found in Psalms 103:8;

> "The LORD is compassionate and gracious, slow to anger, abounding in love." (NIV)

The words compassion, grace, anger and love are all abstract words, ideas that cannot be experienced by the senses. Why do we find these abstract words in a passage from concrete thinking Hebrews? Actually, these are abstract English words used to translate the original

Hebrew concrete words. The translators will often substitute a concrete word for an abstract word because the original Hebrew concrete imagery would make no sense when literally translated into English.

Let us take one of the above abstract words to demonstrate the translation from the concrete into the abstract. Anger, an abstract word, is actually the Hebrew word "אף" (aph) which literally means "nose," a concrete word. When one is very angry, he begins to breath hard and the nostrils begin to flare. A Hebrew sees anger as "the flaring of the nose (nostrils)." If the translator literally translated the above passage "slow to nose," the English reader would not understand.

While the uses of abstract thoughts are commonplace to us and we read them freely without notice, it is essential to see the concrete thoughts behind the abstract thoughts of the translations so that the original meaning of the text can be seen. These abstract thoughts would be as foreign to the author of the text as the idea of being "slow to nose" is to us. As we continue searching for the original meanings of the names of God, we will discover how the ancient Hebrews understood God in a concrete fashion.

El

To uncover the original meaning of the Hebrew word "אל" (el) we will begin by looking at the original pictograph script as we did with the word "חד" (hhad). The pictographic form of "אל" is "𐤀𐤋" where the first picture is the head of an ox, while the second is a shepherd staff.

Ancient Hebrews were an agricultural people raising livestock such as oxen, sheep and goats. The strongest and most valuable of these is the ox. Because of its strength, it was used to pull large loads in wagons as well as to plow the fields. The letter “𐤀” represents the concrete idea of “muscle” and “strength.”

A shepherd always carried his staff. It was a sign of his authority and was used to lead the sheep by pushing or pulling them in the correct direction as well as to fight off predators. Since the yoke is also a staff that is used to direct the oxen, the yoke is seen as a staff on the shoulders (see Isaiah 9:4). The letter “𐤋” represents the concrete view of a yoke as well as leadership from the shepherd who leads his flock with the staff.

When the two letters are combined, the parent root “𐤋𐤀 / אל” (el) is formed with the meaning of an “ox in the yoke” as well as a “strong authority.” It was common to place two oxen in the yoke when pulling a plow. An older, more experienced ox was matched with a younger inexperienced one so that the younger would learn the task of plowing from the older. This older “ox in the yoke” is the “strong leader” of the pair and was the ancient Hebrews concrete understanding of “God.” God is the older ox who teaches his people, the young ox, how to work.

Besides the pictographic evidence for the meaning of the word “אל,” the historical record supports the idea that the original meaning of “אל” is an ox. A Biblical example is found Exodus chapter 32.

> "‘And he [Aaron] took from their hands [the gold earrings] and formed a an idol

> made into a small bull, and they said; 'Israel, this is your God who brought you up out of the land of Egypt.' And Aaron saw it and built an altar before it and Aaron called out saying 'tomorrow is a feast to the LORD."
> Exodus 32:4,5

In this passage, Israel formed an idol of the LORD in the image of a bull. Why did Israel choose a bull for its idol? Many ancient cultures worshiped a god in the form of a bull. The Egyptians name for their bull god is "Apis" and the Sumerians called him "Adad." The Canaanites, whose language is very similar to the Hebrews worship "אל" (el) a bull god.

The word "אל" is frequently translated as God, the "strong authority" of Israel, such as in the following passages.

> "Blessed be Abram by God Most High, Creator of heaven and earth."
> Genesis 14.19 (NIV)

> "For the LORD your God, is God of gods, and Lord of lords, the great God, mighty and awesome."
> Deuteronomy 10:17 (NIV)

When the reader of the Bible sees the English word "God" (beginning with the upper case "g"), it is always applied to the Creator of the heavens and the earth. The Hebrew word "אל" can refer to this same God, but as the concrete understanding of the word "אל" is a "strong and mighty one," this same Hebrew word can be applied to anyone or anything that functions with the same characteristics as seen in the examples below.

> "I [Laban] have the power to harm you"
> Genesis 31.29 (NIV)
>
> "When he rises up, the mighty are terrified."
> Job 41:25 (NIV)
>
> "The mountains were covered with its shade, the mighty cedars with its branches."
> Psalms 80.10 (NIV)
>
> "Your righteousness is like the mighty mountains."
> Psalms 36.6 (NIV)
>
> "Do not worship any other god"
> Exodus 34:14 (NIV)

The imagery of the ox and shepherd staff were common symbols of strength, leadership and authority in ancient times. Chiefs and kings commonly wore the horns of a bull on their head as a sign of their strength and carried a staff representing their authority over their flock, the kingdom. Both of these symbols have been carried through the centuries to the modern day where kings and queens carry scepters and wear crowns. The Hebrew word "qeren", meaning horn, is the origin of the word "crown."

Eloah

The child root "אלה" (eloah), derived from the parent root "אל" (el), encompasses the more specific meaning of the "yoke that binds." This word is usually translated as an "oath," the binding agreement between two parties when entering into a covenant relationship. The oath binds the two parties together, who promise to uphold the terms of the agreement, just as the yoke between the two oxen that are bound together by the yoke.

> "And they said, 'we see that the LORD is with you and we said please, let there be a binding yoke between us, between us and you and let us make a covenant with you'".
> Genesis 26:28

Remembering that the yoke binds the older ox with the younger, the word "אלה" (eloah) can also be used for the older who teaches the younger through the yoke. God, the creator of heaven and earth, is the older ox who has bound himself to the younger ox, his covenant people. Through the covenant, God has bound himself to them in order to teach and lead them through life and into truth.

> "Look, happy is the man whom God corrects and the discipline of God Almighty you do not despise."
> Job 5:17

Elohiym

The word "אלה" (eloah) is made plural by adding the suffix "ים" (iym) to the end of the word, forming the plural word "אלהים" (elohiym), and is used for "strong leaders that are bound to another" as can be seen in the following passages.

> "You shall have no other gods before me."
> Exodus 20:3 (NIV)

> "Then his master must take him before the judges."
> Exodus 21:6 (NIV)

This plural word is also used for the Creator of the heavens and the earth and is the most common word translated as "God" in the Bible and is found in the first verse of the Bible.

> "In the beginning God created the heavens and the earth."
> Genesis 1:1 (NIV)

Due to a lack of understanding of the Hebrew language's use of the plural, many misconceptions and misunderstandings have been introduced into theology based on the use of this plural word "אלהים." One such misconception is the belief that "angels" created the heavens and the earth, choosing to translate the above verse as:

"In the beginning gods (angels) created the heavens and the earth."

While this verse appears to be a literal reading of the text, because of the use of the plural suffix, it is incorrect. The verb in this verse is "ברא" (bara) and would be literally translated as "he created," a masculine singular verb. If the subject of the verb, "אלהים" was in fact a plural, the verb would have been written as "בראו" (bar) and would be literally translated as "they created," a masculine plural verb. Since the verb is singular, the word "אלהים" (elohiym) is singular in number, but is understood as being qualitatively plural rather than quantitatively plural.

The English language, as well as other Western languages, uses the plural to identify quantity, such as two "trees." The ancient Hebrew language on the other hand uses the plural to identify quality as well as the quantity. For instance, the Hebrew language can say "two trees" identifying the quantity, as well as "one trees," identifying its quality as being larger or stronger than the other trees.

Let us look at a couple of scriptural uses where the same plural word is used to express quantity as well as quality. The Hebrew word "בהמה" (behemah) is a "land animal." Hebrew is a gender sensitive language; therefore every word is identified as either masculine or feminine. The suffix "ים" (iym) is used for masculine words while the suffix "ות" (ot) is used for feminine words. The word "בהמה" (behemah) is feminine and would be written as "בהמות" (behemot) in the plural form. Notice the use of this word as it is found in the book of Job.

> "However, please ask the <u>animals</u> and they will teach you, and the birds of the sky and they will tell you."
> Job 12:7

> "Please look at the <u>behemoth</u> which I made with you."
> Job 40:15

In the first verse, the word "בהמות" (behemot) is used in a quantitative manner identifying more than one animal. The second verse uses the same plural word, which most translations transliterate as "behemoth," as some unknown excessively large animal. In this instance, the plural identifies the animal as qualitatively larger than the average "בהמה" (behemah).

The Hebrew word "אלהים" (elohiym) is used in the same sense. It can be used to identify more than one "אלה" (eloah) or one "אלה" (eloah) that is qualitatively stronger, more powerful than the average "אלה" (eloah). The God who created the heavens and the earth is not just a god, but the all-powerful God, mightier than any other god.

> "For the LORD your God (אלהים), he is God (אלהים) of the gods (אלהים), and Lord of lords, the great God (אל), mighty and awesome."
> Deuteronomy 10:17

The Yoke of Jesus

> "Come to me, all who are weary and burdened, and I will give you rest. Take

> my yoke upon you and learn from me, for I am gentle and humble in heart, and you will find rest for your souls. For my yoke is easy and my burden is light."
> Matthew 11:28-30 (NIV)

Jesus asks his followers to yoke themselves to him by following his teachings. Jesus is drawing on this imagery of the older ox that bears the burden of the yoke and teaches the younger.

Chapter 6 - El Shaddai

"And when Abram was ninety nine years old and the LORD appeared to Abram, and he said to him, I am *El Shaddai,* walk before me, and be perfect."
Genesis 17:1

Before examining the word Shaddai, let us take a moment to discuss some of the problems with Biblical translations.

Translations

There are many factors that go into a translation which are invisible and unknown to the reader of a translation. Most Bible readers assume that the English translation of the Bible is an equivalent representation of the original text. Because of the vast difference between the ancient Hebrews' language and our own, as well as the differences in the two cultures, an exact translation is impossible. The difficult job of the translator is to bridge the gap between the languages and cultures. Since the Hebrew text can be translated many different ways, the translator's personal beliefs will often dictate how the text will be translated. A translation of the Biblical text is a translator's interpretation of the original text based on his own theology and doctrine. The reader is then forced to use the translators understanding of the text as his foundation for the text. For this reason, readers will often compare translations, but are usually limited to Christian translations. I always recommend including a "Jewish" translation when comparing texts, as this will give a translation from a different perspective. Yes, it will be biased toward the Jewish faith, but Christian translations are biased toward the Christian faith as well. A comparison of the two translations can help to discover the bias of each.

The translator's task is compounded by the presence of words and phrases whose original meanings have been lost. In these cases the translator will attempt to interpret the words and phrases as best as possible based on the context of the word and the translators opinion of what the author was attempting to convey. When the reader of the translation comes across the translator's attempts at translating the difficult text, the reader makes the assumption that the translator has accurately translated the text. The following passage will give an adequate example of some of the difficulties the translators face when attempting to convert the text into an understandable English rendering.

> "Make a roof for it and finish the ark to within 18 inches of the top. Put a door in the side of the ark and make lower, middle and upper decks."
> Genesis 6:16 (NIV)

The above translation seems very clear, concise and understandable. The reader would have no problem understanding the meaning of the text and assumes that this translation adequately represents the original text. Behind this translation lies the Hebrew, which must be a translator's nightmare. Below is a literal rendering of the same verse according to the Hebrew.

> "A light you do to an ark and to a cubit you complete it from to over it and a door of the ark in its side you put unders twenty and thirty you do."

This is not an isolated case, but occurs continually throughout the Biblical texts. In order to assist the English reader, the translator has supplied words, phrases and even whole sentences to enable the reader to understand the text. The reader is rarely aware of the difficulties in translating a certain passage and assumes that the translator has accurately translated the text.

To demonstrate how a Translator's interpretation of a text can influence the readers understanding of the text, let us examine two passages from the New International Version.

> "Let the land produce living creatures."
> Genesis 1:25

> "and the man became a living being."
> Genesis 2:7

From these passages the reader could conclude that animals are classified as "creatures" and humans as "beings" (The KJV uses the word "soul" here). When the Hebrew text is uncovered, we find that the above "interpretation" would never have occured as we find that the phrase "living creature" in the first verse and the phrase "living being" in the second verse are two different translations of the same Hebrew phrase "nephesh chayah". Because of the translator's opinion that there is a difference between men and animals, the translation of these verses reflects the translator's opinions. The reader, not knowing the Hebrew background to the passages, is forced to base his interpretation on the translator's personal opinion.

In the previous chapter we have discussed the meaning of the word "אל" (el), as found in "אל שדי" (el shaddai), and will now focus on the word "שדי" (shaddai). Most Bible translations translate this word as "Almighty." Many times a translator will not translate a Hebrew word literally because the literal meaning would mean nothing to the Western mind, and in some cases would actually be offensive to the Western reader. Such is the case with the word "שדי" (shaddai). The use of the word "Almighty" by the translator is his attempt at translating the text in a manner that will both make sense to the Western reader as well as retain some of the meaning of the original Hebrew word.

The parent root for this word is "שד" (shad). The original pictographs for this word are, "ㅠш." The "ш" (sh) is a picture of the two front teeth and has the meaning of "sharp," "press" (as from chewing) as well as "two." The "ㅠ" (d) is a picture of a tent door with a meaning of "hang" or "dangle" as the door is hung or dangles down from the top of the tent.

The combined meanings of the "ш" and "ㅠ" would be "two danglers." The goat was a very common animal within the herds of the Hebrews. It produces milk within the udder and is extracted by the goat kid by squeezing and sucking on the two teats dangling below the udder. The function of these teats is to provide all the necessary nourishment for the kids, as they would die without it. The Hebrew word "שדי" (shaddai) also has the meaning of a "teat." Just as the goat provides nourishment to its kids through the milk, God nourishes his children through his milk and provides all the necessities of life. This imagery can be seen in the following passage:

> "And I will come down to snatch them [Israel] from the hand of the Egyptians and to bring them up from that land to a good and wide land to a land flowing with milk and honey."
> Exodus 3:8

The word "שדי" (teat) is often coupled with the word "אל" (mighty, strong) creating the phrase "אל שדי" (el shaddai) literally meaning the "mighty teat," hence we can see the translator's reluctance to literally translate this phrase in this manner and instead using the more sanitized "God Almighty."

Mother

The idea of God being characterized as having teats does not sit well in our Western culture. We are familiar with identifying with God as a father, but not as a mother.

The Hebrew word for mother is "אם" (em) or "𐤀𐤌" in the ancient pictographic script. The ox head meaning "strength" combined with the picture for "water" (𐤌) forms the word meaning "strong water." Animal's hides were placed in a pot of boiling water. As the hide boiled, a thick sticky substance formed at the surface of the water and was removed and used as glue, a binding liquid or "strong water." The mother of the family is the "one who binds the family together."

God can be seen as the "glue" that holds the whole universe together. This is more than a figurative statement but also very scientific. All matter is composed of atoms, which consist of protons with a positive charge and electrons with a negative charge. The protons are packed together in the nucleus, the center of the atom, while the electrons orbit the nucleus. Since each proton has a positive charge, each proton should repel the others causing the protons to fly apart, but for some unknown reason, they do not. This phenomenon is called "nucleic bonding." God literally "binds" the entire universe together.

> "male and female he created them ".
> Genesis 1:27 (NIV)

This passage states that man was created as male and female and also that man was created in the image of God. God has the characteristics of both male and female and these characteristics were put in man, the male characteristics were placed in men while the feminine characteristics were placed in women. When a man and a woman come together, they unite these characteristics as one, now a perfect representation of God.

> "and they shall become one flesh."
> Genesis 2:24 (NIV)

God promised the nation of Israel that he would bring them into a "land flowing with milk and honey." God as the "אל שדי" (el shaddai), the mighty teat, will supply his children with his life sustaining milk.

Chapter 7 - Yahweh

"This is the history of the heavens and the earth, in the day of creation *Yahweh* God made the land and heavens"
Genesis 2:4

When reading the Bible, the reader will come across the word "lord" written two different ways such as in the following verse:

> "O LORD, our Lord, how majestic is your name in all the earth."
> Psalms 8:1 (NIV)

The first use of the word lord is written in all upper case letters while the second uses the upper case for the first letter only. While the same English word is used for both, the Hebrew words behind them are very different. Unfortunately, most readers gloss over these words without even a thought to the actual Hebrew words or their meanings.

The next chapter will discuss the meaning of the Hebrew word that is translated as "Lord," while here we will look into the meaning of the Hebrew behind "the LORD." Wherever this word appears in the English text, in all upper case letters, it is the Hebrew name of God, "יהוה" (YHWH), often called the Tetragrammaton. Anyone who has done even a cursory study on this name has discovered that there is much debate on the actual meaning and pronunciation of the name.

In order to appreciate the complexity in reconstructing the pronunciation and meaning of the name, it will be necessary to go through the history of the written form of the name through the centuries.

History

We know that in ancient times this name was used and pronounced throughout the history of the Old Testament as we can see in the following passages.

> "And he built there an altar to YHWH (יהוה) and he called on the name of YHWH (יהוה)."
> Genesis 12:8

> "My soul will praise YHWH (יהוה), the humble ones will hear and they will rejoice. I will make great YHWH (יהוה) and we will lift up his name together."
> Psalms 34:2,3

The name was originally written as "𐤉𐤄𐤅𐤄" in the Hebrew pictographic script. When Israel was taken into Babylonian exile in 597 BC, they found the Aramaic square script easier to write and adopted it for writing Hebrew. At this point the name was written as "יהוה." The square Aramaic script adopted by Israel is the same script used today to write Hebrew.

Sometime between the exile and the first century A.D. the use of the name יהוה fell into disuse. It no longer was acceptable to pronounce the name of יהוה, as it was deemed too holy to pronounce. Israel also believed that the actual pronunciation of the name could not be known for certainty. In order to prevent a mispronunciation of the name, they elected not to pronounce the name. This non-use of the name was based, in part, on the command found in the Ten Commandments.

> "You shall not lift up the name of YHWH (יהוה) your God falsely because YHWH (יהוה) will not consider innocent anyone who lifts up his name falsely."
> Exodus 20:7

It became common during this time to use a different word, called a euphemism, as a replacement for the name. Some of the more common "euphemisms" were "adonai" (my lord), "hashem" (the name), "shamayim" (heaven) and "hagibur" (the power). Over time, these euphemisms also began to be used to replace other names of God such as "אלהים" (elohiym). Some of these euphemisms can be seen within the New Testament writings such as can be seen in one of Jesus' parables that is recorded in both Matthew and Luke.

> "And another parable put he forth unto them, saying, The Kingdom of <u>heaven</u> is like to a grain of mustard seed, which a man took, and sowed in his field: which indeed is the least of all seeds: but when it is grown, it is the greatest among herbs, and becometh

> a tree, so that the birds of the air come and lodge in the branches thereof."
> Matthew 13:31,32 (KJV)

> "Then said he, unto what is the kingdom of God like? And where-unto shall I resemble it? It is like a grain of mustard seed, which a man took, and cast into his garden; and it grew and waxed a great tree; and the fowls of the air lodged in the branches of it."
> Luke 13:18,19 (KJV)

In this parable you will notice that Matthew uses the phrase "kingdom of heaven" while Luke uses the phrase "kingdom of God." This same difference of phraseology can be seen throughout these two books. The phrase "kingdom of heaven" has mistakenly been interpreted to be a kingdom located in heaven, because the euphemism was not understood. The phrase 'kingdom of heaven" is synonymous with "kingdom of God" where "heaven" is a euphemism for "God." "Heaven" is not a place, but a person, God.

Matthew's gospel was obviously written to an audience familiar with the euphemism, most likely the Jewish community. Luke, on the other hand, wrote his gospel to a community, probably of Gentiles, that would not have been familiar with the euphemism, and therefore used the more literal phrase "Kingdom of God."

The second use of a euphemism in the New Testament is found in Matthew's account of Jesus' trial before Caiaphas the High Priest where the euphemism "power" is used in place of "God" or "YHWH".

> "Jesus saith unto him, Thou hast said: nevertheless I say unto you, Hereafter shall ye see the Son of man sitting on the right hand of power, and coming in the clouds of heaven."
> Matthew 26:64 (KJV)

A third use can be seen in a New Testament quotation of an Old Testament passage. Here the Hebrew name "יהוה" is replaced with the word "Lord."

> "A voice of one calling in the wilderness prepare the way of YHWH (יהוה), make straight in the wilderness the road of our God."
> Isaiah 40:3

> "For this is he that was spoken of by the prophet Esaias, saying, The voice of one crying in the wilderness, prepare ye the way of the Lord, make his paths straight."
> Matthew 3:3 (KJV)

During the first century, continuing to this day, the reader of the Hebrew Scriptures would see the name "יהוה," but would replace it with a euphemism and read it as "adonai" (Lord). It is interesting to note that it is this word, "Lord," that all the Christian Bibles have also chosen to use to replace the name "יהוה."

A new development in the Hebrew language occurred around 700 AD. Many of the written words in the Hebrew language contained no vowels and were only known by tradition. Over time this caused a wide variation in pronunciations. The Masorites invented a system for adding vowels to the text in order to aid and standardize pronunciation. These vowels were written as dots and dashes placed above and below the Hebrew letters. Below is the text of Genesis 1:1 as it would appear without the vowels followed by the sounds represented by the letters:

בראשית ברא אלהים את השמים ואת הארץ

brashyt bra alhym at hshmym wat harts

Below is the same text with the addition of the vowels and the resulting pronunciation:

בְּרֵאשִׁית בָּרָא אֱלֹהִים אֵת הַשָּׁמַיִם וְאֵת הָאָרֶץ

bereshiyt bara elohiym et hashamayim w'et ha'arets.

When the Masorites came to the name YHWH, they had a dilemma, how do you add vowels to a word where the pronunciation is not known, and, as they understood it, a sin to pronounce incorrectly? Their decision was to take the vowels from the Hebrew word "אדוני" (Adonai - Lord), the standard euphemism for "יהוה," and place them in the name "יהוה" (YHWH) as shown below.

יְהוָֹה אֲדוֹנָי

This is how the name "YHWH" appears today in any Modern Hebrew Bible. The vowels were not placed in the name to give it pronunciation, but for the reader to recognize the vowels as coming from the word "adonai". When the reader comes across this name, it is read as "adonai".

Pronunciation

Many possible pronunciations for this name have been proposed over the centuries, some of the more common ones are Jehovah, Yahveh, Yahweh and Yahueh. While the actual pronunciation cannot be determined with complete accuracy, there are some clues within the Biblical text that can assist with the pronunciation of the name. Let us begin by looking at each letter individually.

The first letter in the name is the Hebrew letter "yud." The Modern Hebrew pronunciation of this letter is "Y." In ancient Hebrew this letter doubled as a vowel and could be pronounced as a "Y" or an "I."

The second and fourth letters of the Hebrew name "YHWH" is the Hebrew letter "hey." The modern pronunciation is "H." In the ancient Hebrew language this letter was a consonant/vowel and could have the pronunciation of "H" or "E."

The third letter is, in Modern Hebrew, the letter "vav." While the modern pronunciation is "V," the ancient pronunciation was "W" which, is retained in the Arabic language, a sister language of Hebrew. While the Hebrew pronounces the name "David" with a "V," the Arabic pronunciation is "Dawid." This letter is also a consonant/vowel and can also be pronounced as "W," "U" or "O."

Below is a chart with all the possible pronunciations for the letters in the name "YHWH":

Hebrew	Sound
י	Y, I
ה	H, E
ו	W, O, U
ה	H, E

In order to find the original pronunciation, we will need to examine the various uses of the name throughout the Old Testament.

It was common for Hebrew names to have alternate spellings. For example the name "אליה" (Eliyah/Elijah - my God is YH) was also written as "אליהו" (Eliyahu - my God is YHW) . The same is true for the name "יהוה" (YHWH) which has the shortened form "יה" (YH) as found in some passages.

> "My soul will bless YHWH (יהוה), Praise YH (יה) ".
> Psalms 104:35

The Hebrew pronunciation of "praise YH" is "hallelu-YH" (as in Halleluyah), where the traditional pronunciation of "YH" is "yah." The name "Eliyah," meaning "my God is YH" is another use of the shortened form of the name "YHWH". It is clear that the traditional pronunciation of the first part of the name is "yah." The name Eliyahu has retained the pronunciation of the third letter in the name "YHWH" as a "U." We now have the pronunciation "yahu" for the first three letters of the name.

The final letter "H" could have been pronounced as a consonant "H," in which case it would be silent, or as the vowel "E," pronounced "ey." This gives us two possible pronunciations of "YHWH", Yahuh or Yahuey. It is possible that the name may have had several alternate pronunciations, just as the name Eliyah/Eliyahu. These pronunciations would be "Yah," "Yahuh" and "Yahuey."

Another possibility for the name is "Yahweh" and is commonly used today. The only difference between this pronunciation and the one proposed above is the consonantal pronunciation of the letter "ו" is used rather than the vowel pronunciation.

As the actual pronunciation cannot be positively determined, the pronunciation "Yahweh" will be used in the remainder of this book for the Tetragrammaton. This pronunciation is more commonly used than the other pronunciations proposed here and it is more consistent to the Hebrew letters than the more common pronunciation of Jehovah.

Jehovah

Probably the most commonly known and used pronunciation of the name "YHWH" is "Jehovah", which came about through a series of misunderstandings and mistakes. Around the 16th century a German Biblical scholar came across the Hebrew name "יְהֹוָה" in the Hebrew text and attempted to pronounce it, unaware of the history of the vowel points added to the name.

The letter "J" is a recent addition to the Latin alphabet and a history of this letter is necessary for understanding how this letter became a part of the pronunciation of "YHWH". When the Hebrew names of the Old Testament were first transliterated into Latin, the Latin letter "I" was chosen to transliterate the Hebrew letter "Yud." The Latin letter "I" could be pronounced as the consonantal sound "Y" or the vowel sound "I," just as the Hebrew letter "yud" could have a "Y" or "I" sound. In the 14th century AD the letter "J" was introduced into the Latin alphabet and was used interchangeably with the letter "I." By the 16th century the "J" became standardized with a "Y" sound, while the "I" was standardized with the "I" sound. It was not until the 17th century that the Latin "J" took on the pronunciation that we are familiar with today.

To demonstrate the progression of the Latin transliteration of the Hebrew letter "yud," we will follow the progress of the name "Jacob" from its original Hebrew to modern English in both written and spoken form.

Alphabet	**Written**	**Spoken**
1st Century Hebrew	יעקב	Ya'akob
14th Century Latin	Iacob	Yacob
16th Century Latin	Jacob	Yacob
17th Century English	Jacob	Jacob

When the name "יְהוָֹה" was transliterated into German, it became "Jehovah", but pronounced as "Yehovah." When the word "Jehovah" is read in modern English, it becomes the pronunciation Jeh-ho-vaw, as known to us today.

While the pronunciation of a name is important, it should not have the emphasis that many groups have placed on it. Many times a different language or even a dialect cannot pronounce certain sounds; therefore, the pronunciation of a word or name will vary. It is not the pronunciation of the name through which the person is revealed, but the character that is represented in the name. For this reason we will now examine the meaning of the name "YHWH".

Meaning

The name "יהוה" (Yahweh) comes from the Hebrew root "היה" (hayah). This root and the words derived from it can have a wide variation in meaning and application. The original concrete meaning is "breath" and has the extended meaning "exist," as one who exists, breathes. The name "Yahweh" is parallel with this root in Exodus chapter 3 where God introduces himself to Moses.

> "And God said to Moses ehyeh asher ehyeh (אהיה אשר אהיה - I exist whom I exist), and he said; you will say this to the sons of Israel, ehyeh (אהיה) sent me to you. And God said again to Moses; you will say to the sons of Israel, Yahweh, the God of your fathers, the God of Abraham, The God of Isaac, and the God of Jacob sent me to you, this is my name forever and this is how I will be remembered from generation to generation."
> Exodus 3:14,15

Through Hebrew poetry, the name "יהוה" is being paralleled with the verb "אהיה." Both of these words are identified as names that Moses is to take to Israel. From this we can conclude that the name "יהוה" has the meaning of "breath." Interestingly, all the letters in both words, "יהוה" and "אהיה," are vowels that are pronounced with a "breath." We can see a close similarity between the pronunciation of the letters themselves and the meaning of the word.

As we have previously seen, the spirit in Hebrew thought is the breath. Just as the breath of man cannot be seen but is essential for life to exist, Yahweh also cannot be seen but it is his breath in man that gives him life.

> "And YHWH (יהוה) God formed the man of dust from the ground and he blew into his nostrils the breath (נשמה) of life and the man hayah (היה breathed/existed) as a living soul."
> Genesis 2:7

Chapter 8 - Lord

For Yahweh your God is God of the gods and *Lord* of the lords, the great and mighty
Deuteronomy 10:17

In the previous chapter we looked at the word "LORD," in all upper case letters as found in most English translations. In this chapter we will look at the same word when used in lower case letters. In most cases, the Hebrew word "אדן" (adon) lies behind the English word "lord." It is used throughout the Bible and is used commonly in prayer, but the actual meaning of the word is through the translation having robbed it of its cultural meaning.

Again we will begin our search for the Biblical meaning of "אדן" (adon) by looking at its parent root "דן" (dan). In the ancient pictographic script, this word would have appeared as "𐤃𐤍." Both of these letters have been discussed previously, the letter "𐤃" (d), is a door meaning "to enter" and the letter "𐤍" (n), is a seed meaning "perpetual life." When these letters are combined we find the Hebraic definition, "the door of life" or "to enter a perpetual life."

One child root derived from this parent is "דין" (diyn), meaning to "judge." This word is used as a legal term, but not in the modern Western sense of seeking guilt or condemnation, rather it is seeking innocence or life from an Eastern Hebraic sense. We can see this search for innocence in Genesis 15:4 where God punishes the guilty in order to bring life to the descendents of Abraham who were unjustly treated as slaves.

> "But I will punish the nation they [the descendents of Abraham] serve as slaves, and afterward they will come out with great possessions." (NIV)

In the next two passages, the word "דין" (diyn) is paralleled with "save," meaning to deliver from a trouble or burden and "compassion." Just as a deliverer saves ones life from an enemy, a judge also brings life (diyn).

> "God, in your name save me, and in your might judge me."
> Psalms 54:1

> "For Yahweh will judge his people, and on his servants he will have compassion."
> Psalms 135.14

We have seen that the parent root "דן" (dan) means "to enter life" and the child root "דין" (diyn) is "to bring life to another." We now come to the child root "אדן" (adon - lord) which means "one who brings life" or "one who opens the door to perpetual life," the judge or deliverer. In the ancient Hebraic culture each family was a kingdom unto itself, the head of the family, the patriarch, was the king. Within the hands of this king was the power to take or grant life and for this reason he is seen as the "אדן" (adon). After Jacob flees from his family, Esau becomes the head of the family, he is the "אדן." When Jacob returns he is afraid for his life and approaches Esau as a servant in the hopes that Esau will spare his life.

> "And you are to say, it is an offering from your servant Jacob sent to my lord (אדן) Esau and he is coming after us."
> Genesis 32:18

Moses is also called "אדן," the deliverer and judge of Israel.

> "And Joshua son of Nun, attendant of Moses from his youth, answered saying, my lord (אדן) Moses stop them."
> Numbers 11:28

As Genesis 1:1 states:

> "In the beginning God created."

All life is granted by God which makes him "אדן" over all creation.

> "And the angel answered saying, these are the four spirits of heaven going out from the standing over the lord (אדן) of all the earth."
> Zechariah 6:5

The Lord gives names

In the ancient world it was custom for the lord to name those who are under him. Such is the case in Daniel chapter one where the chief official of King Nebuchadnezzar (identified as lord in 1:10) changes the names of four Hebrew slaves.

> "Among these were some from Judah: Daniel, Hananiah, Mishael and Azariah. The chief official gave them new names: to Daniel, the name Belteshazzar; to Hananiah, Shadrach; to Mishael, Meshach; and to Azariah, Abednego."
> Daniel 1:6,7 (NIV)

Several other times names are changed such as, Abram and Sarai to Abraham and Sarah (Genesis 17:5,15) and Jacob to Israel (Genesis 32:28). The most common reason given for the change in a name is a change in character of the individual, since, as we have seen, ones character is reflected in his name.

In the case of Abraham, this is not true for reasons that I will detail here. Abraham's original name is' "אברם" (Abram) formed by combining the two words, "אב" (abh) and "רם" (ram). God then changed this name to "אברהם" (Abraham), also formed by combining two words, "אב" (abh) and "רהם" (raham). The word "אב" (abh) means "father" and is the first part of both names. The difference between the two names is the second syllable, from "רם" (ram) to "רהם" (raham). The word "רם" (ram) means "high," "lifted up" or "exalted." The word "רהם" (raham) is not found in the Bible except in this name only.

While no one is certain of the meaning of the second part to the name "אברהם" (Abraham), scholars have proposed the meaning of "father of a great multitude" supposedly from combining the two words "רב" (rabh), meaning "many" or "great," and "הם" (ham), meaning "multitude." To shorten "רב הם" (rabh ham) into the word "רהם" (raham) is very unlikely as dropping a consonant such as the "ב" (b) completely removes the original meaning of the word and is not a practice in Hebrew word construction.

A more plausible explanation is that the word "רהם" (raham) is the original word, being a child root from the word "רם" (ram), meaning "high" or "lifted," as found in the original name of "אברם" (Abram). Several other child roots are derived from "רם" including; "ארם" (aram), "ראם" (ra'am), "הרם" (haram), "רום" (rum) and "ירם" (yaram), all of which also mean "high" or "lifted up." From this we can conclude that the child root "רהם" (raham) would have the same meaning of "high" or "lifted up."

If "אברם" (Abram) and "אברהם" (Abraham) both mean "father lifted up," the reason for the change in the name is not due to a change in the character of Abraham. What then would be the reason for the change in name?

In Genesis chapter one, God, the lord over all creation gives the names to the creation including: the day and night (1:5), the sky (1:8) and the land and seas (1:10). In Genesis Chapter two, Adam (A Hebrew word meaning man) gives names to all of the animals, birds and beasts (2:21,22) and we are told that Adam will rule over these animals, birds and beasts (1:26, 28). Adam also names his wife (2:23) and we are told that he is to rule over her as well (3:16). From this we discover that in the Hebraic mind, the one who gives the name is the lord over the one has been given the name. This same scenario is repeated throughout the scriptures. The founder, or lord, of a city gives the name of the city, the father, lord of the family, gives names to his children, even the gods created by men are named by the men in the hopes of having lordship over the gods. We also see this in our original discussion of the change of the Hebrew slaves named by the chief official of King Nebuchadnezzar who now has lordship over them.

Abram was given his name by Terah, his father and lord. It is not until after the death of Terah that God changes Abram's name to Abraham, not because of a change of character in Abram, but because of a change in lordship. God is now claiming lordship over Abraham. Abraham does not name his son, but God himself (Genesis 17:19) does, showing that God was the lord of Isaac from birth. Interestingly, out of the three patriarchs Abraham, Isaac and Jacob, Isaac is the only one named by God from birth and whose lifespan is the longest. Jacob was named by his father Isaac, but changed by God (Genesis 32:28 and 35:10), to Israel after the death of his father. Both John the Baptist (Luke 1:13) and Jesus (Matthew 1:21 and Luke 1:31) were named by God through an angel (see the next chapter for more on "the angel of the Lord") rather than by their parents.

Chapter 9 - Angel

The *Angel* who redeemed me from all evil
Genesis 48:16

The word "מלאך" (mela'ak) is translated two different ways as can be seen in the following examples.

> "And they sent a messenger unto Joseph, saying, Thy father did command before he died, saying. . . .."
> Genesis 50:16 (KJV)

> Behold, I [Yahweh] send an Angel before thee, to keep thee in the way, and to bring thee into the place which I have prepared."
> Exodus 23:20 (KJV)

The word "מלאך" (mela'ak) is formed by adding a "מ" (m) in front of the child root "לאך" (la'ak). The child root "לאך" is derived from the parent root "לך" (lak) or "ШJ" in the ancient pictographic script. The "J" (l), as we have seen, is a staff, while the "Ш" (k) is a picture of the palm of the hand. The parent root "ШJ" has an original Hebraic meaning of "staff in the palm" or "to walk," as a staff was a common tool carried by the traveler. Two other child roots formed from "לך," "הלך" (halak) and "ילך" (yalak) mean "to walk" as well. The word "מלאך" (mela'ak) is "one who walks for another," a "messenger."

This can be one who walks for another man, and translated as "messenger" as seen in the first verse above. This word can also be one who walks for God, and translated as "angel" as seen in the second verse.

When Jacob blessed his son Joseph, he calls God a "מלאך" (mela'ak - messenger/angel). Jacob uses the common Hebrew poetry of parallelism by repeating his declaration that God is his deliverer and redeemer in three separate ways:

> "The God who my fathers Abraham and Isaac walked before,
> The God who shepherded me from the beginning to this day,
> The Angel who redeemed me from all evil. . . .."
> Genesis 48:15,16

God is able to send himself as his own messenger which can also be seen in the following summary of God's promise to lead the nation of Israel into the promised land:

The Angel leads Israel

> "And I [Yahweh] will come down to snatch them from the hand of the Egyptians and to bring them up from that land to a good and wide land to a land flowing with milk and honey."
> Exodus 3:8

God hears the cries of Israel's bondage in Egypt and promises he will bring them out and lead them into the

Promised Land. Once Israel is delivered and taken into the wilderness, Israel begins to grumble and complain. When Yahweh meets Moses at the burning bush, he tells Moses of his plan for Israel. Yahweh delivers them out of Egypt and brings them to Mount Sinai. Throughout this journey Israel grumbles and complains and Yahweh becomes angry with them.

> "Look, I [Yahweh] will send a messenger (מלאך) before you to guard you on the way and to bring you to the place which I prepared. Be on guard from his face and hear his voice, do not make him bitter he will not forgive your rebellion for my name is within him."
> Exodus 23:20,21

> "And I [Yahweh] will send before you a messenger (מלאך) and he will cast out the Canaanites, the Amorites and the Hittites and the Peruzites the Hivites and the Jebusites, to a land flowing with milk and honey for I will not go up with you because the people are stiff necked and I will turn and devour you on the way."
> Exodus 33:2,3

After God declares that his "Angel" will lead them into the Promised Land, we read that it is Yahweh who will go before them preparing their way into the land.

> "And they will say to the dwellers of this land, as they have heard, that you

Yahweh are within this people who saw you Yahweh, eye to eye, and your cloud stood over them and you walked before them in the pillar of cloud by day and in a pillar of fire by night. "
Numbers 14:14

"And in this thing you did not believe in Yahweh your God who walked before you on the way to search for you a place to camp, in a fire by night to show you the way you are to walk and in a cloud by day."
Deuteronomy 1:32,33

"And you will know today that Yahweh your God is the one who will cross over before you as a devouring fire, he will destroy them and he will subdue them before you."
Deuteronomy 9:3

It would appear from the above passages that Yahweh promises to take Israel into the Promised Land but because of their stiff necks, Yahweh says that he will not go but will send his "messenger." Then we read that Yahweh himself goes before them to prepare the way to the Promised Land. Again, we have Yahweh who does not go with them but it is the "messenger" Yahweh who does. Another apparent contradiction concerning Yahweh is found in Exodus chapter thirty-three:

> "And Yahweh spoke to Moses face to face, just as a man speaks to his friend."
> Exodus 33:11

> "And he [Yahweh] said, you cannot see my face because man cannot look on it and live . . . And when my glory passes by, I will set you in a cleft of the rock, I will cover over you with my palm until I pass by. I will remove my palm and you can see my back, but my face you cannot see."
> Exodus 33:20,22,23

It is important to make a distinction between the simple reading and understanding of any text from ones interpretation of the text. It is not uncommon for people when reading the text to make an interpretation of the text based on their preconceived beliefs and biases. When we read the Bible and interpret it according to our beliefs, we will never discover truths within it and therefore we are unable to grow in understanding. Instead, we must learn to read the Bible according to what it says and adjust our beliefs according to what the text says.

The simple reading of the above text states that Moses spoke with Yahweh face to face but Moses was not allowed to see the face of Yahweh. There are many different ways to interpret this apparent contradiction, and it is not my intention to do so here, but only to point out that according to the texts, there is a "messenger" of Yahweh called Yahweh.

We will now look at another series of passages where the "messenger of Yahweh" is not only called Yahweh, but also God.

The Angel of the Lord

> "And Moses was shepherding the flock of Jethro his father-in-law, the priest of Midian and he drove the flock to the back of the wilderness and he came to Horeb the mountain of God. And he saw the messenger of Yahweh (יהוה מלאך) in flames of fire from the middle of the bush. And he saw and looked, the bush was consumed in fire and the bush was not devoured."
> Exodus 3:1,2

Throughout the scriptures this "messenger of Yahweh" appears to individuals such as we see with Moses' encounter at the burning bush. Is this "messenger" a specific angel or God himself? In this passage, as can be seen in other passages as well, we will see that Yahweh is his own messenger.

> "And Yahweh saw that he turned to see and God called to him from the middle of the bush and he said, Moses, Moses. And he said, I am here. . . . And he said, I am the God of your fathers, the God of Abraham, the God Isaac and the God of Jacob. And

> God hid his face because he was afraid to look at God."
> Exodus 3:4,6

The "messenger of Yahweh" is now identified as God, the God of his fathers. Moses knew that this was God for he was afraid to look at his face, knowing that anyone who looks at the face of God would die (Exodus 33:20).

> "And God again said to Moses, Say to the sons of Israel, Yahweh, the God of your fathers, the God of Abraham, the God of Isaac and the God of Jacob."
> Exodus 3:15

We have now seen that the "messenger of Yahweh" is God. In the above passage we see that Yahweh is God. From this we can conclude that the "messenger of Yahweh" is actually Yahweh himself.

Chapter 10 - King

For God is <u>King</u> over all the earth
Psalms 47:7

In this chapter we will look at the Hebrew word "מלך" (melek), an adopted root word. The original parent root is "לך" (lak) which we previously discussed as the root for "מלאך" (mela'ak - messenger), one who "walks for another." At some point the "מ" (m) was attached to the original root, forming the adopted root "מלך" (melek). The ancient pictographic form of the letter "מ" is "𐤌," a picture of water meaning mighty, due to the immense size of the sea. The Hebraic understanding of the word "מלך" (melek) according to the ancient script is "a mighty one who carries a staff in the palm." The king was a mighty man who carried a scepter, or staff, as a sign of his authority. The pictographs for the word also mean, "a mighty one that walks." The ancient kings did not rule by sitting on a throne his entire life, distancing himself from the people, rather he ruled among them, he walked with them. The king also lead the army into battle as King Josiah did when he was killed. God is not a king who merely sits on his throne, but one who walks among his people.

> "For Yahweh himself walks among your camp."
> Deuteronomy 23:15

Covenant

We have previously looked at the word "אלה" (alah) meaning an oath or covenant. The more common Hebrew word for a "covenant" is "ברית" (beriyt) from the parent root "בר" (bar) meaning grain. The grain is fed to the livestock for fattening. These fat animas were then used for sacrifices. Whenever a covenant was entered into, such as between a king and his people, a fatted animal was cut into two pieces. The blood was then sprinkled on the parties of the covenant. Where the English phrase "made a covenant" appears, we find the Hebrew phrase "כרת ברית" (karat beriyt) behind it. This phrase is literally translated as "cut the fatted meat." Essentially the two members of the covenant are saying by this cutting "if I break this covenant you may do the same to me," as can bc seen in the following passage.

> "The men who violated my covenant, who did not lift up my words of the covenant which they cut before me, I will make them like the calf that they cut into two and passed between."
> Jeremiah 34:18

Throughout the Bible we see God as the king, making covenant with his people. In these covenants both parties agree to the terms of the covenant. In the case of the covenant God makes with Israel at Mount Sinai, God promises to provide for them as a good king, while the people agree to obey the laws of the king.

Keeping Covenant

The Bible often refers to the keeping and breaking of a covenant and it is usually interpreted as obedience or disobedience to the covenant. If disobedience were the meaning of "breaking," Israel would never have been able to remain in covenant relationship so long as they did because of their continual disobedience to the terms of the covenant. Let us examine these two words within their Hebraic context beginning with the word for "keep":

> "Now, if you will intently listen to my voice and keep my covenant, they will be for me a treasured possession from all the people, for all the land is mine."
> Exodus 19:5

In the above passage, the Hebrew word behind the English word "keep" is "שמר" (shamar). If we interpret this word as obedience, we can easily interpret this passage to mean, "obey the covenant." As we shall see, this translation is not always suitable to the context of the passage.

> "The LORD bless you and keep you."
> Numbers 6:24 (NIV)

Obviously the word "שמר" (shamar), also translated as "keep" in this verse, cannot be interpreted as "obey," otherwise it would read, "The LORD bless you and obey you." We can clearly see that the word "obey" is a poor interpretation for the Hebrew word "שמר" (shamar).

The original use of this word is a corral constructed out of thorn bushes by the shepherd to protect his flock from predators during the night. The "שמר" (shamar) was built to "guard" the flock and we can see this same imagery in the passage above by interpreting it as "The LORD bless you and guard you." We now see that "keeping the covenant" is not strictly about obedience, but "guarding the covenant." The individual's attitude toward the covenant is the issue, does he guard it as a shepherd does his flock, or does he "break" the covenant.

Breaking Covenant

Just as the word "keep" has been misunderstood in the context of the original Hebraic meaning, the word "break" has also been misunderstood, as the word does not mean "disobedience."

> "If you reject my decrees and if you cast away my judgments and you do not do all my commands, breaking my covenant, then, I will do this to you; I will bring upon you sudden terror, disease and fever."
> Leviticus 26:15,16

The Hebrew translated as "break" in the above passage is "פרר" (parar). The original use of this word was the "treading" over grain. The harvested grain was thrown onto the threshing floor where oxen would trample over the grain breaking the hull open, releasing the edible seeds inside. The "breaking" of a covenant is the total disrespect for the covenant where one literally throws it to the ground and tramples on it. As we can see, the keeping and breaking of a covenant is the respect, or lack of, that one has for the covenant.

Servants

Within a kingdom there are two types of people, subjects and servants. The subjects, usually called "the people," confine their activities and passions to their family and for the most part are oblivious to the needs and desires of the king. The servant on the other hand is continually occupied with the needs and wishes of the king. His sole purpose in life, his passion, is to recognize and fulfill the needs, desires, wishes and will of the King. A good servant will learn from and study the king so that he knows the king so well that he can anticipate the needs and wishes of the king. A servant knows what the king wants because the will of the master is in him; the servant becomes "אחד" (ehhad - one) with the king.

The Hebrew word for a "servant" is "עבד" (ebhed) from the root "עבד" (abhad) meaning to "serve." Note the two different translations of this one Hebrew word.

> "We will worship the LORD at his sanctuary with our burnt offerings sacrifices and fellowship offerings."
> Joshua 22:27 (NIV)

> "The LORD God took the man and put him in the Garden of Eden to work it and take care of it."
> Genesis 2:15 (NIV)

The Western mind has separated our lives into two parts; secular "work" and holy "worship" and each are approached in different ways. The Eastern mind does not make this distinction and sees both "work" and "worship" as "עבד" (abhad). The cleaning of a restroom is just as much a service to the king as singing praises to the King from a choir. Our service to the king should include all aspects of life.

> "So whether you eat or drink or whatever you do, do it all for the glory of God.."
> 1 Corinthians 10:31 (NIV)

> "Worship the Lord your God, and serve him only."
> Matthew 4:10 quoting Deuteronomy 6:13 (NIV)

Chapter 11 - Father

You Yahweh, are our *Father,* our redeemer, forever is your name
Isaiah 63:16

The Hebrew word for father is "אב" (abh), a parent root, and written as "בא" in the ancient pictographic script. As we have previously discussed, the first letter is an ox head representing strength and the second is the tent representing the family that resides within the tent. They have the combined meaning of the "strength of the tent," the poles which stand tall and firm supporting the tent itself. The father is also the one who stands tall and firm supporting the family.

Action words

This brings us to another difference between the ancient Hebrew Eastern culture and our modern Western culture. In Western languages, a noun simply identifies a person place or thing, while the verb describes the action of a noun. The noun itself is void of any action. As an example, the nouns "knee" and "gift," in a Western culture, are inanimate objects void of any action in themselves.

The ancient Hebrews were an active and passionate people who saw action in all things and their vocabulary reflects this lifestyle. In the Hebrew language, just as in most ancient languages, very little distinction was made between nouns and verbs as all words were related to action. The Hebrew verb "ברך" (barak) means "to bend the knee," the noun "ברך" (berek) means "a knee that bends." Notice that both words are spelled exactly the same in Hebrew, with the only difference being the vowels that are supplied to them. When a word is used as a verb it is used to describe the action of something, while when used as a noun, it describes something that has action.

The verb "ברך" is usually translated as "bless," but as this is an abstract word, the more Hebraic concrete meaning is "to come with a bent knee." This can be literal or figurative as seen in the following two verses.

> "Come worship and bow down and <u>bend the knee</u> (literal) before Yahweh our maker."
> Psalms 95:6

> "Yahweh will give strength to his people, Yahweh will <u>bend his knee</u> (figurative) with peace to his people."
> Psalms 29:11

When this word is understood in its original Hebraic meaning, the passages in the Bible come more alive. Such as we can see with our Hebraic definition of father, the one who stands firm supporting the family.

Son

Too often we see our relationship with God by looking at him as a lofty King that sits on a throne while we are the subjects far below. God designed the family structure in order to teach us the true relationship between God and his children.

The Hebrew word for son is "בן" (ben) or in the ancient script "𐤁𐤍." This word is Hebraicly understood as "the tent continues." The "𐤁" as a representation of the tent and the "𐤍" as a representation of the seed that continues with the next generation. This word can also mean, "the household continues." The Hebrew mind saw the "tent" and the "sons" as the same thing as they both function in the same manner.

The tent was constructed of woven goat hair. Over time the sun bleaches and weakens the goat hair necessitating its continual replacement. Each year a new panel, approximately 3 feet wide and the length of the tent, is made by the women. The old panel is removed and the new strip is added to the tent. In the same manner, the family is continually renewed by the birth of sons, also "made" by the women. As the family grows through the birth of more sons, the tent is required to be made larger and additional panels are added. This is the imagery found in Isaiah 4:2 which is speaking about women who have born no children (vs. 1):

> Enlarge the place of your tent, stretch your tent curtains wide, do not hold back; lengthen your cords, strengthen your stakes. (NIV)

Just as the panels of the tent turn white by the sun and are replaced, the hair of the elderly members of the family turn white. They are removed through death and replaced by new members, the sons. To identify the age of an individual we say, "he is fifty years old." The Hebrew idiom for this is to say "he is a son of fifty years." This could also be translated as "he is fifty panel changes" as one's age can be calculated by the number of panels changed during his lifespan.

The child root "בנה" (banah) derived from the parent root "בן" (ben), literally means "to build a house." The house (tent) is built with panels (בן) while the household is built with sons (בן).

> "And Jacob left Succoth and he built (בנה) a house."
> Genesis 33:17
>
> "And she [Rachel] said, here is my maidservant Bilhah, come to her and she will bear a child over my knee and I will also build (בנה) from her."
> Genesis 30:3

The father builds his family through his sons who will one day replace him. It is the responsibility of the father to teach and instruct his sons in family matters so that when the time comes for them to lead the family, they will do so according to the will of their father. A Hebrew word meaning "to instruct" is "בין" (beyn), another child root from the parent root "בן (ben). The father builds his house by raising and instructing sons.

As the sons of God, it is our responsibility to listen and learn from our father who is in heaven so that we can grow to follow in his will.

> "My desire is to do your will my God, and your teaching is within my heart."
> Psalms 40:8

In the above passage, the "teaching" of God is paralleled with his "will." This brings us to another Biblical word, "תורה" (torah) that is commonly misunderstood.

The Teachings

The Hebrew word "תורה" (torah), while usually translated as "law," is not "law" but "teaching as can be seen in the following verses.

> "Listen, my son, to your father's instruction and do not forsake your mother's <u>teaching</u>."
> Proverbs 1:8 (NIV)

> "My son, do not forget my <u>teaching</u>, but keep my commands in your heart."
> Proverbs 3:1 (NIV)

To fully understand the Hebraic meaning of the word "תורה" (torah) we will begin with the parent root, "יר / [illegible]" (yar). The letter "[illegible]" (Y) is a hand and the letter "[illegible]" (R) is a man. These two letters form the parent root meaning the "hand of man" or "to throw."

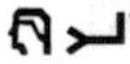

The child root "ירה" (yarah) is the throwing of an object such as a stone, arrow or the finger that is thrown in a direction one is to walk, to point. This latter meaning of "to point" can either be a literal pointing toward a physical direction, or a figurative pointing to a teaching that is to be followed. From this child root "ירה" (yarah), two Biblical words are derived, "מורה" (moreh) and "תורה" (torah).

The Hebrew word "מורה" (moreh) is "one who throws." This can be a teacher (or father) who throws (points) his finger in a direction the student (or son) is to take. It can also be an archer who throws an arrow at a target.

The Hebrew word "חטא" (chata) means "to miss the mark," as when the archer misses his target. This word is also used when the student, or son, misses his target or direction. In this last case, the word "חטא" (chata) is translated as "sin." Sin is to miss the target, which our heavenly father has pointed out to us.

The second word derived from "ירה" (yarah) is "תורה" (torah) meaning "what is thrown by the thrower (moreh)." This can be the arrow of the archer, or the direction pointed by the teacher or father.

To translate the Hebrew word "תורה" (torah) as "law" would be the same as translating the word "father" as "disciplinarian." While a father is a disciplinarian, it is not all that the father is. In the same way, there is law within the torah but that is not all that torah is. Law is a "static set of rules and regulations established by a government to a people where violations are punished." Torah is a "dynamic set of instructions established by the father to his children where disobedience is disciplined through correction and punishment, but obedience is praised."

A father teaches his children how to live a life that is right, healthy and prosperous. God is the father who instructs his children with the same teachings.

> "Blessed is the mighty man who you discipline, Yahweh, and from the torah you teach us."
> Psalms 94:12

Love

> "You shall love Yahweh your God with all your heart, with all your mind, and with all your resources."
> Deuteronomy 6:5

When reading the word "love" our mind usually equates this with an emotional feeling. To understand the Hebrew concept of love, "אהב" (ahabh) in Hebrew, we will examine the parent root as well as its derivatives. The parent root is "הב" (habh) written as "[pictograph]" in the ancient pictographic script. The "[pictograph]" is a man holding his arms out as if saying, "look at that." The "[pictograph]" is the outline of the Hebrew nomadic tent. Based on the pictographs of the parent root we have the meaning of "look at the house."

Derived from the parent root are two child roots. The first is "יהב" (yahabh) meaning "to give as a gift or a privilege."

> "And Jacob said to Laban, give my wife to me."
> Genesis 29:21

> "Rachel saw that she bore no children for Jacob and Rachel was jealous of her sister and she said to Jacob, give me children so that I will not die."
> Genesis 30:1

> "Give to Yahweh, sons of gods (mighty ones) give to Yahweh glory and strength."
> Psalms 29:1

The family into which one is born is seen as a privilege given as a gift. The children born to the parents are seen in the same manner; the wife as well is given as a privilege to the husband as marriages were usually arranged within the ancient cultures. The second child root is the word "אהב" (ahabh). While usually translated as love, the Hebraic meaning is "the care of the gift." It is the family members responsibility to teach, provide, cherish and protect the other members of the family.

> "And Isaac brought her to the tent of his mother Sarah and he took Rebecca to be his wife and he loved her."
> Genesis 24:67

> "And Jacob loved Rachel."
> Genesis 29:18

As we can see "אהב" (ahabh) is not an emotion, but an action, a responsibility. One that you did not choose but were given as a privilege to be a part of. The father sees his wife and children as the gifts of God, which he is responsible to care for. The wife and children were also given the father as a gift and their responsibility is to care for him as well. With this frame of mind, the family becomes "אחד" (ehhad - one). When we read that we are to "love God," it is not an emotion but a responsibility to listen and learn from him and walk in the teachings that he has given to us, we then become "אחד" (ehhad - one) with our heavenly father.

> "Listen Israel, Yahweh is our God, Yahweh is One. You shall <u>love</u> Yahweh your God with all your heart, with all your mind, and with all your resources."
> Deuteronomy 6:4,3

Chapter 12 - Savior

For I am Yahweh your God, the holy one of Israel, your *Savior*
Isaiah 43:3

The parent root which will lay the foundation for the words in this chapter is "שע" (sha'). The pictographic form of this word is "ꟹш." The first letter is a picture of the two front teeth that are "sharp" for cutting. The second letter is an eye used for "watching." Combined they mean, "sharp watching." The Hebraic background of this word, and the child roots formed from it, is a shepherd who sharply or intently watches over his flock.

The shepherd is continually watching the area for dangerous terrain or waters that may be hazardous to the flock as well as keeping an eye out for predators that may attack the flock. The shepherd carries the weapons of his trade, a staff for striking and a sling for throwing deadly round stones. When one from the flock is attacked, the shepherd jumps to his defense and repels the invader, rescuing the sheep. God is frequently compared to a shepherd as he also watches over his flock and delivers them from trouble.

"Yahweh is my shepherd"
Psalms 23:1

Delight

The word "שעשע" (sha'ashua) is formed by doubling the parent root, a common means of intensifying a word, and is translated as "delight." While the word "delight" is an abstract word, the Hebrew requires a more concrete understanding. One carefully watches over those things that he takes delight in. The shepherd takes delight in his flock and therefore, carefully watches over them much as we as parents take delight in our children and carefully watch over them.

> "Your witnesses, men of counsel, intently watch over me."
> Psalms 119:24

> "I long for your rescue Yahweh, your teachings intently watch over me."
> Psalms 119:174

Yahweh as our shepherd continually watches over us with delight. He gives us counselors and teachings that are meant to watch over us and lead us away from troubles. When we, as the sheep, come upon trouble, he is the shepherd who delivers us.

Cry out

Just as the shepherd hears the cry of one from his flock and comes to his rescue, God hears the cry of his people and come to their rescue. This imagery can be seen in God's rescue of Israel from the bondage of the Egyptians.

> "And Yahweh said, I have seen the oppression of my people which are in Egypt and their pleas I have heard because of the task masters, for I know their pain. And I will come down to snatch them from the hand of the Egyptians and to bring them up from that land to a good and wide land to a land flowing with milk and honey."
> Exodus 3:7,8

From our parent root comes the child root "שוע" (shavah) meaning "to cry out."

> "In my trouble I call out to Yahweh and to my God I cry out. He hears my voice from his Temple and my cry came before him in his ears."
> Psalms 18:6

God, as the shepherd of his flock, hears the cries of his sheep, he comes to their rescue delivering them from trouble and oppression.

Salvation

The next child root is "ישע" (yasha) and means "save," "free," "rescue" or "deliver." The shepherd delivers his flock from the enemy and releases them back into the free, wide, open space of the pasture in freedom. The idea of being "saved" to the ancient Hebrew was not a future salvation into the world to come, but an immediate salvation from any enemy, trouble or distress. Throughout the Psalms David cries out to God to save him from his enemies.

> "O LORD my God, in thee do I put my trust: save me from all them that persecute me, and deliver me."
> Psalms 7:1 (KJV)

> "I will call upon the LORD, who is worthy to be praised: so shall I be saved from mine enemies."
> Psalms 18:3 (KJV)

Derived from this child root is the word "ישועה" (yeshuah), and means, "rescue."

> "I long for your rescue Yahweh, your teachings intently watch over me."
> Psalms 119:174

This word is most frequently translated as "salvation" but the concrete understanding of "rescue" is a more Hebraic understanding of the word. When the original context of this word, being a shepherd's "careful watching" and "rescue," is applied to "salvation," we can more clearly see the author's meaning as in the passages below.

> "Truly my soul waiteth upon God: from him cometh my salvation. He only is my rock and my salvation; he is my defense; I shall not be greatly moved."
> Psalms 62:1,2 (KJV)

> "Truly my soul waiteth upon God: from him cometh my <u>salvation</u>."
> Psalms 62:1 (KJV)

Savior

A second word derived from the child root "ישע" (yasha) is "מושיע" (moshia), "one who delivers," or a "deliverer," such as the shepherd who delivers the sheep. During the days of the judges, God raises up deliverers to deliver Israel from the hands of their oppressors, beginning with Othniel.

> "And the sons of Israel called out to Yahweh and Yahweh raised up a <u>deliverer</u> for the sons of Israel And Othniel son of Kenaz, the younger brother of Caleb saved them."
> Judges 3:9

This word is also translated as "savior" (or "saviour" in the old English of the King James Version).

> "and all flesh shall know that I the LORD am thy <u>saviour</u> and thy Redeemer, the mighty one of Jacob."
> Isaiah 49:26 (KJV)

Jesus

> "She will give birth to a son, and you are to give him the name Jesus, <u>because</u> he will save his people from their sins."
> Matthew 1:21 (NIV)

When we read the account of Joseph's encounter with the angel regarding the birth of "Jesus," we are told that there is a connection between the name "Jesus" and the idea that he will "save" his people. Because of the translation, the actual connection is lost.

God sent another Savior, Jesus. As names in our Western world are simple identifiers, the word "Jesus" has no intrinsic meaning. Because of this, the character of Jesus is diminished because the Hebraic meaning of the name has been lost through the translations. A history of how the name "Jesus" appeared will help us understand his function more clearly in a Hebraic sense.

We have discussed the Hebrew word "ישועה" (yeshuah) which means "salvation," or more Hebraicly, "rescue" or "deliver." This word is a feminine word and is made masculine by dropping the final "ה" (h) forming the masculine word "ישוע" (yeshua). This is the original Hebrew name of Jesus.

Through the centuries, the original name of Yeshua evolved into the Latin form "Jesus." When the Greeks transliterated the Hebrew name Yeshua, the "Y" was transliterated into an "I" as Greek has no "Y" sound. The "Sh" was transliterated into an "S" for the same reason. Most Greek names end with an "S": therefore, the "S" replaces the final "A." The result being the Greek name "Iesus," the familiar name found in the Greek New Testament. As we discussed with the name "Jehovah", the "I" sound was written with a "J" in Latin. While the name "Jesus" appears in the Latin text, it was read as "Iesus." Around the 17th Century the "J" became the "J" sound that we are familiar with today and we now pronounce the name as "Jesus."

As the original name of Jesus is "ישוע" (yeshua) from the word "ישועה" (yeshuah), we find that the original meaning of his name is "rescue," a picture of is his character or function. We now see the connection between his name and function.

> "She will give birth to a son, and you are to give him the name Jesus (Yeshua), because he will save (yasha) his people from their sins."
> Matthew 1:21 (NIV)

Command

The word "command" usually brings to mind a meaning similar to "the orders of a general to his troops which are to carried out without question or understanding." This is another case where our Western culture has given an interpretation outside of its Hebraic context. Two related Hebrew words are translated as "command," "צו" (tsav) and "מצוה" (mitsvah), both derived from the parent root "צה" (tsah).

Several other words derived from this parent word will provide the actual Hebraic context that will help us understand the meaning of "command" as understood by the Hebrews. The word "ציי" (tsiyiy) is a "nomad." The shepherds were desert dwellers who traveled through the wilderness in search of water and pastures for the flocks. The Hebrew word "ציון" can mean a "desert" or "landmark." This word is also used as a place name and transliterated as Zion, the holy mountain of God. The nomad uses the various landmarks of the desert much like we use road signs to guide us to our destination. Another word is "יצא" (yatsa) while usually translated as "to come out," is the "migration" or the journeys of the nomad.

The words "צו" (tsav) and "מצוה" (mitsvah) are literally the landmarks that point out the road to green pastures or figuratively the commands that point out the road to life. An interesting parallel can be seen in Israel's journey to the Promised Land where they follow two roads, one literal and the other figurative. God as the shepherd brings Israel out of Egypt on a migration to the Promised Land, literally mount Zion in modern day Jerusalem. On this journey, God takes them through the desert by leading them from landmark to landmark. The second road is the journey of life where God gives the landmarks of morality to follow to bring them to a righteous life.

If a nomad walked hoping to stumble across one of his "landmarks," he would become lost. Often in our walk through life we stumble across a situation that we recognize as an opportunity to perform a "command" of God. Just as the nomad must be actively in search of his "landmarks," we, in the same manner, should be actively searching for applications to the "commands" of God. When we are told to "feed the hungry" or "visit the sick," we are not to stumble across a hungry or sick person, rather we are to be searching for them.

Chapter 13 - Shepherd

Yahweh is my *Shepherd*
Psalms 23:1

Throughout the Bible God is compared to an ox, eagle, king, and a parent, among others, as we have previously discussed. Probably the most common imagery ascribed to God in the Bible is that of a shepherd. In the previous chapter we saw the Hebraic similarities to God as a deliverer and a shepherd. In this chapter we will examine the Hebraic understanding of a shepherd and his interaction with the flock.

The standard Hebrew word for a "shepherd" is "רעה" (ra'ah) derived from the parent root "רע" (ra'). The ancient pictographic form for this parent root is "[pictographic]," the pictures of a man and an eye meaning, "a man watches." As we saw in the last chapter, the shepherd intently watches over his flock, this function can also be seen in this word. This parent root also has the meaning of a "friend." The Shepherd is not a distant ruler or overseer, but a constant companion and friend to the flock. He spends more time with his flock; traveling to watering holes and green pastures, then he does with his own family. Our relationship with God is meant to be this type of relationship, where we become intimate friends with our guardian, protector and provider.

Gathering the flock

The parent root "קל/ᒧ-ɵ-" (qal) is formed by combining the picture of the sun at the horizon, meaning draw in, with the picture of a shepherd staff. The combined meaning is "to draw to the shepherd staff." The child root "קול" (qol) is translated as "voice" and it is the voice of the shepherd that calls the flock to be drawn toward his staff (the sign of his authority). Another child root derived from this parent root is "קהל" (qahal) meaning, "assemble." This word is used throughout the Bible for the "assembly" or "congregation" of Israel, the sheep who hear the voice of their shepherd Yahweh.

> "These words Yahweh spoke to all your assembly (קהל - a gathering flock) with a great voice (קול - voice of the shepherd) from in the midst of the fiery cloud on the mountain."
> Deuteronomy 5.22

In this passage we can clearly see the imagery of the shepherd calling his sheep. When the voice of Yahweh (the shepherd) came from the mountain, all of Israel (the sheep) gathered in front of the mountain (the staff) to hear his words.

Yeshua also identifies himself as the shepherd who calls his sheep.

> "My sheep listen to my voice; I know them, and they follow me. I give them eternal life, and they shall never perish;

> no one can snatch them out of my hand."
> John 10:27,28 (NIV)

Yeshua and his Assembly

Around 250 BC, the Old Testament was translated into a Greek text called the Septuagint. These translators used the Greek word ekklesia meaning, "assembly," to translate the Hebrew word "קהל" (qahal). This same Greek word is also found throughout the New Testament and is translated into English as "church."

> "And I tell you that you are Peter, and on this rock I will build my church (ekklesia/qahal - the assembly of sheep)."
> Matthew 16.18 (NIV)

The church that Yeshua calls to himself is his flock which he watches over, protects and provides for. As the shepherd, he is also the friend and companion to the flock.

Discipline

We are going to look at four Hebrew words that impart the idea of "discipline." When looking at these words from a Hebraic perspective we are able to see into the Hebrews' world and how they saw the concept of "discipline" with a concrete understanding.

From the parent root "לם" (lam - shepherd staff), the ancient name for the letter "ל/𐤋" (L), comes the adopted root "למד" (lamad - shepherd staff), the modern Hebrew name for the letter "ל/ᒍ" (L). Both words mean, "shepherd's staff," which the shepherd always carries for guiding, leading and protecting the flock. This staff was also used to push or pull one from the flock that is not following the correct path.

> "The day that you stood before Yahweh your God in Horeb, In his speaking to me, assemble (קהל) before me the people and they will listen to my words that they will learn (למד) to fear me all they days that they live over the land and they will also cause their sons to learn (למד)."
> Deuteronomy 4:10

This form of discipline is the pushing and pulling of the student/son/sheep toward the correct direction that he is to take.

The second word is "אלף" (alaph) which is literally the yoking together of two oxen. This word is also an adopted root and is from the parent root "אל" (el) discussed previously, meaning ox. The younger ox learns from the older ox, to which he is yoked. This form of discipline is learning by association where the student/son learns by watching and working along side the teacher/father. This can also work in a negative sense as in the following passage.

> "Do not make friends with a hot-tempered man, do not associate with one easily angered, or you may learn

(אלף) his ways and get yourself ensnared."
Proverbs 22:24,25 (NIV)

The next word is "יסר" (yasar) from the parent root "סר/" (sar). The pictographs in this root are a thorn, which causes one to turn from its pain, and the head of a man. Combined they mean, "to turn the man." This form of discipline is a chastising with blows or words to cause the student/son to change directions.

> "Discipline (יסר) your son, and he will give you peace; he will bring delight to your soul."
> Proverbs 29:17 (NIV)

The last word is "שנן" (shanan). This word literally means, "to sharpen." In order for a knife to be sharp it must be carefully and consistently run across a stone. This form of discipline is the sharpening of skills by the student/son. The duties and responsibilities given to the student/son foster the learning of the necessary skills to survive.

> "These commandments that I give you today are to be upon your hearts. Impress (שנן) them on your children. Talk about them when you sit at home and when you walk along the road, when you lay down and when you rise up."
> Deuteronomy 6:6,7 (NIV)

God uses these four principles of discipline on us; his children. We are to learn them from him, follow his methodology and likewise raise our children in a godlike manner.

Chapter 14 - Creator

The everlasting God Yahweh is the *Creator* of the ends of the earth
Isaiah 40:28

A "creator" is theologically understood as, "one who makes something out of nothing." The Hebrew word used in the introductory passage, translated as "creator," is "בורא" (borey), literally meaning "one who fattens." Without an understanding of the cultural background of this word, the idea of God "fattening" the heavens and earth is as foreign to our Western mind as the idea of creating something from nothing is to the ancient Hebrews. As we have previously discovered, the Hebrews always view their world with a concrete mind rather than an abstract mind. A "creator" or "one who creates" is an abstract thought which the ancient Hebrews would have had no way of comprehending.

Through our modern Western perspective, we have read the story of creation as an account of God's miraculous creation of the universe by his command, the reason for which being unclear. This is not the concept that the author of Genesis chapter one implies in the language of the ancient Hebrews. This misconception begins with the Hebrew word "ברא" (bara) as found in the first verse of the chapter.

> "In the beginning God <u>created</u> the heavens and the earth."
> Genesis 1:1 (NIV)

The word "ברא" (bara), translated as "created" above, comes from the parent root "בר" (bar) which we have previously discussed, meaning "grain." The grains were very important staples to the Hebrews. They were used in making breads and feeding the livestock. This parent root also has the meaning of "fat" as livestock fed on grain become fat. The child root "ברא" (bara), also means, "fat" as seen in the following verse.

> "And the ugly cows that looked thin ate the seven beautiful cows that looked <u>fat</u>."
> Genesis 41:4

A "fat" cow is one that is "full"; therefore, "ברא" (bara) Hebraicly can mean, "to fill." When we read the first two verses of Genesis from a Hebraic perspective we can see this imagery clearly.

> "In the beginning God <u>filled</u> the sky and the land because the land was empty and unfilled."
> Genesis 1:1,2

This "filling" up of the sky and land is also described in the days of creation, which are written in true Hebrew poetry. The first three days of creation describe the separating of the skies and the land, this is paralleled with the last three days that describe the "filling up" of the skies and the land.

The first day is the separation of light and darkness and parallels the fourth day where the light and darkness is filled with the sun and moon. The second day is the separation of the water and the sky, it parallels the fifth day where the water and sky are filled with fish and birds. The third day is the separation of water and land and it is paralleled with the six day where the land is filled with the animals and man.

The word "בורא" (borey) is derived from the child root "ברא" (bara) and literally means "one who fills" rather than "creator." As we see in the Creation story, God is the one who fills the waters, skies and the land.

Chapter 15 - Jealous

For Yahweh, whose name is *Jealous,* is a *Jealous* God
Exodus 34:14

From a Western perspective, the idea of one being named "Jealous" seems odd, especially as a name for God. As a name represents the character, this implies that God is by nature jealous. Our cultural understanding of the word is a type of anger felt over the suspected unfaithfulness of a spouse. As we shall see the Hebrew word has a very different meaning.

Nest

The parent root "קן/ᓄ-ѳ-" (qen) is a nest.

> "Like an eagle he wakes up his nest, over his chicks he hovers, he spreads his wings, he takes them, he carries them over his feathers."
> Deuteronomy 32.11

The first letter of the parent root is a picture of the sun at the horizon where the light is gathered during the sunrise or sunset. The second letter is a sprouting seed, the beginning of new life that came from the parent plant. Combined, these letters form the meaning, "A gathering for the seeds." A bird goes about "gathering" materials for building a nest for her "seeds," eggs, of the next generation.

Several words are derived from the parent root "קן" (qen - nest), all related in meaning to the building of a nest.

Builder

The child root "קנה" (qanah) is the construction of a nest by the parent bird.

> "And he blessed him and he said blessed is Abram to God most high, builder of heaven and earth."
> Genesis 14:19

Some translations translate the above verse as, "Creator of heaven and earth." The ancient Hebrews did not see God as an unknowable force that creates the universe for some unknown reason; rather he is the bird that goes about gathering all the necessary materials for building a home for his children. Man was not created as an additional component to the creation; the earth was created as a home for man.

Guard

Another word derived from "קן" (qen) is "קנא" (qana). This is the word translated as "jealous" in our introductory passage. The Hebraic meaning of this word is the passion with which the parent guards over the chicks in the nest. While our Western mind may see the term a "jealous God" in his feelings and actions toward us, it is in fact his feelings and actions toward our enemies. The heathens and false gods are like predators invading the nest and God fights them protecting his children from their clutches.

Chapter 16 - Everlasting

Before the mountains were born and you began the land and the earth, from *everlasting* to *everlasting,* you are God
Psalms 90:2

The Hebrew word "עולם" (olam) is often translated as eternal, everlasting or forever, all of which have a meaning of a "continual existence," an existence without end. Again, this concept misses the meaning of the original Hebrew. The ancient Hebrew mind would not concern himself with what is beyond his known world. Anything that is beyond his world, or beyond his understanding, is "beyond the horizon," the actual meaning of the Hebrew word "עולם". When David says that God is "עולם", he is acknowledging that God is beyond his understanding.

Notice that the introductory passage repeats the word everlasting twice. The ancient Hebrew language has no way to say that something is "best" or "greatest." Instead the Hebrew language doubles a word to give it emphasis such as in the passage above. God is not just "beyond the horizon"; he is "far beyond the horizon."

Chapter 17 - Holy

Be *holy* for I, Yahweh your God, am
holy
Leviticus 19:2

The word holy is another abstract word used to translate the Hebrew word "קדוש" (qadosh) from the root "קדש" (qadash), also commonly translated as "holy." The Hebraic meaning of this word is lost due to the preconception of the English word "holy" which implies one who is exceptionally pious and righteous. The word "קדש" (qadesh), equivalent to the word "קדש" (qadash), is translated differently in other places, which will clearly show that "קדש" (qadash) does not mean holy in the commonly perceived sense.

> "No Israelite man or woman is to become a temple prostitute."
> Deuteronomy 23:17 (NIV)

We would never consider a "prostitute" as holy and yet the Hebrew word "קדש" (qadesh) is translated as a "temple prostitute." The literal meaning of "קדש" (qadash) can be seen below.

> "Take the anointing oil and anoint the tabernacle and everything in it; consecrate it and all its furnishings, and it will be holy."
> Exodus 40:9 (NIV)

Furniture are inanimate objects that cannot be holy, pious or righteous, but they can be "set apart for a specific function," the true meaning of "קדש" (qadash). These can be the furnishings of the Temple that are used for this purpose alone, or a prostitute whose is set apart from the rest of society for a specific purpose. The children of God are set apart from all others; they have the specific function of living for God and showing the world who God is.

God is set apart from all other gods.

> "There is none <u>holy</u> like Yahweh for there is none beside you and there is no rock like our God."
> 1 Samuel 2:2

Conclusion

The breath of God, his character or his name, functions within a unity. Throughout the Bible we see different manifestations of God. Some of these we have discussed, such as the fire that gives warmth, the cloud that gives shade, the ox that teaches, the bird that protects its young, the lord who brings life and the shepherd that protects the flock. These all work together in harmony to protect and provide for his people. While God has many names, he only has one name. The many characteristics of God function in unity. The ultimate purpose of this book is not only to show the characteristics of God, but also to show the potential characteristics of man.

The filling of man

> "So God created man in his own image, in the image of God created he him; male and female created he them."
> Genesis 1:27 (KJV)

While the above is a common translation for this verse, there are two words within it, that when translated from a Hebraic perspective, illuminate the passage in a new light. The first word is "ברא" (bara), which in this verse cannot mean, "create something from nothing," as another verse would contradict this translation.

> "And Yahweh formed the man from the dust of the ground and blew into his nostrils the breath of life."
> Genesis 2:7

God did not create the man out of nothing; instead he formed him out of the ground. With our new understanding of the word "ברא," discussed previously, he filled him with his image, which brings us to the next word.

The word "צלם" (tselem), translated as "image" above, is also translated in other passages as an "idol," which is an "image" of a god. A more Hebraic understanding of the word would be a "shadow." An idol is meant to be a "shadow" of the original, a representation, just as a "shadow" is the image of the original. We can now read the above passage as:

> "So God filled the man with his shadow, with the shadow of God he filled him; male and female he filled them."
> Genesis 1:27

Man was formed from the dust of the ground, but unlike the other animals, man was filled with the shadow of God. All that God is we were made to duplicate, just as a shadow duplicates the original. Genesis 2:7, quoted above, states that man was filled with God's breath, therefore, the shadow of God is the same as his breath. From our previous discussion on the word "נשמה" (neshemah - breath), we see that God filled the man with a shadow of his breath, his character.

The whole character (neshemah/shem/name) of man is meant to function as a shadow of God, a representative of his character. God filled us with his own character; he has placed his name within us. If we gain a clearer understanding of the character, or name, of God, we have a clearer understanding of our own character, or name. For this reason, it is essential that we have a good name, a name that will direct others to the name of all names.

> "A good name is more desirable than riches, silver and gold."
> Proverbs 22:1

Yeshua

> "He is the image of the invisible God."
> Colossians 1:15 (NIV)

> "I tell you the truth, the Son can do nothing by himself; he can do only what he sees his Father doing, because whatever the Father does the Son also does."
> John 5:19 (NIV)

Yeshua came as the full representation of God; his life can be characterized as a perfect shadow of God, following in the footsteps of his father. His character, while unique in that no other individual has manifested the characteristics of God in such a perfect way, is not meant to be unique. He came to teach us our full potential, so that we can follow in his steps and even to surpass them.

"I tell you the truth, anyone who has faith in me will do what I have been doing. He will do even greater things than these, because I am going to the Father."
John 14:12 (NIV)

The character of God in man

Within scripture we see individuals who manifest the same characteristics as God and we can see some of these in our own lives and have the potential to manifest them all.

The father of the household manifests many of the characteristics of God to his family. He is the "אל" (el - power), the older experienced ox that is yoked to his children to teach them. As the "אדון" (adon - lord) of the family it is his responsibility to bring life to the family through his own work, teaching and decision-making. He is the "מלאך" (mela'ak - messenger), whose responsibility is to bring the messages of God to his family. He is the "מושיע" (moshia - deliverer) of his family by protecting them from evil, both literal and figurative. As "בורא" (borey - creator) he creates new life. He is the "קנה" (qanah - jealous one) by guarding over his family. He is to be "קדוש" (qadosh - set apart) from the world and devoted to God and his teachings.

Appendix A

Hebrew Alphabet

Name	Sound	Script	Picture	Meaning
Aleph	a[1]	א	Ox	strong, lead
Beyt	b, bh[2]	ב	Tent	family, in
Gimel	g	ג	Foot	gather, walk
Dalet	d	ד	Door	move, enter
Hey	h,e[3]	ה	Arms up	look, breath
Waw[4]	w,o,u	ו	Tent peg	add, secure
Zayin	z	ז	Mattock	food, cut
Hhet	hh[5]	ח	Tent wall	outside, half
Tet	t	ט	Basket	contain, mud
Yud	y, i[6]	י	Hand	work, throw
Kaph	k, kh[7]	כך[8]	Palm	bend, tame
Lamed	l	ל	Staff	teach, bind, to
Mem	m	מם	Water	chaos, mighty
Nun	n	נן	Seed	continue
Samech	s	ס	Thorn	hate, protect
Ayin	gh[9]	ע	Eye	watch, know
Pey	p, ph	פף	Mouth	blow, edge
Tsade	ts	צץ	Man's side	hunt, lay down
Quph	q	ק	Sun	condense,circle
Resh	r	ר	Man's head	first, top
Shin	sh, s	ש	Teeth	sharp, two
Tav	t	ת	Cross	mark, signal

1. This letter is silent in modern Hebrew but was originally the vowel sound “a.”

2. Pronounced as a “v.”

3. While an “H” sound only in modern Hebrew, it was also the vowel “e” in ancient Hebrew.

4. While modern Hebrew recognizes this letter as a “vav” with a “v” sound, its original name was “waw” with a “w” sound.

5. The sound “Hh” sound is guttural and hard, as in the German word “ich” or the name “Bach.”

6. While a “Y” sound in modern Hebrew, it was also the vowel “i” in ancient Hebrew.

7. The sound “Kh” is guttural and hard as in the German word “ich” or the name “Bach.”

8. Five letters in the modern Hebrew alphabet include two forms, the first is the form used when at the end of a word, the second is used at all other times.

9. This letter is silent in modern Hebrew but originally had a soft “g” sound as the “g” in English.

Bibliography

Ancient Alphabets and Inscriptions

- "Writing," Smith's Bible Dictionary, 1987 ed.: 327.
- "Alphabet," The New Westminster Dictionary of the Bible, 1976 ed.: 30.
- "Writing," NIV Compact Dictionary of the Bible, 1989 ed.: 632-3.
- "Archeology and the Bible," The Lion Encyclopedia of the Bible, 1986 ed.: 38.
- "Writing," The New Harper's Bible Dictionary, 1973 ed.: 829.
- E. Raymond Capt, Missing Links Discovered in Assyrian Tablets (Thousand Oaks, Ca.: Artisan Sales, 1985) 24, 44.
- Ernst Doblhofer, Voices in Stone (New York, Viking Press, 1961) 35
- Emily Vermeule, Greece in the Bronze Age (Chicago, Ill. The University of Chicago Press, 1964)

Hebrew Culture

- William Smith, Smith's Bible Dictionary (Grand Rapids, Mi.: Zondervan, 1948)
- J.I. Packer, Merril C. Tenney, William White, Jr., Nelson's Illustrated Encyclopedia of Bible Facts (Nashville: Thomas Nelson, 1995) Madelene S. Miller and J. Lane Miller, Harper's Bible Dictionary, (New York, Harper, 1973)
- Merrill F. Unger, Unger's Bible Dictionary, (Chicago, Moody, 1977)

- Henry H. Halley, Halley's Bible Handbook (Grand Rapids, Mi: Zondervan, 24th)
- The New Westminster Dictionary of the Bible (Philadelphia, Westminster, 1976)
- NIV Compact Dictionary of the Bible, (Grand Rapids, Zondervan, 1989)
- The Lion Encyclopedia of the Bible, (Tring England, Lion, new rev. ed.1986)
- Fred H. Wright, Manners and Customs of Bible Lands (Chicago: Moody, 1983)
- Madeleine S. Miller and J. Lane Miller, Encyclopedia of Bible Life (New York: Harper & Brothers, 1944)
- Holman Bible Dictionary, (Nashville, Holman, 1991)
- Mary Ellen Chase, Life and Language in the Old Testament (N.Y., W. W. Norton and Company Inc. 1955)
- Emmanuel Anati, Palestine before the Hebrews (N.Y., Alfred A. Knopf, 1963)
- Donald Powell Cole, Nomads of the Nomads, (Arlington Heights, Ill., Harlan Davidson, Inc., 1975)

Word Studies

- James Strong, New Strong's Concise Dictionary of the Words in the Hebrew Bible, (Nashville, Nelson, 1995)
- W. E. Vine, Merrill F. Unger, William White, Vine's Expository Dictionary of Biblical Words, (Nashville, Nelson, 1985)
- Benjamin Davidson, The Analytical Hebrew and Chaldee Lexicon, (London, Samuel Bagster)
- Ehud Ben-Yehuda, David Weinstein, English-Hebrew Hebrew-English Dictionary, (N.Y., Washington Square Press, Inc., 1961)

Hebrew Thought

- Mary Ellen Chase, Life and Language in the Old Testament (N.Y., W. W. Norton and Company Inc., 1955)
- Thorleif Boman, Hebrew Thought Compared with Greek (N.Y., W.W. Norton and Company, 1960)
- Jeff A. Benner, The Ancient Hebrew Language and Alphabet (Reading, Pa. Ancient Hebrew Research Center, 00)

Hebrew Language

- Gesenius' Hebrew Grammar, (London, Oxford Press, 2nd English Ed. 1910)
- William R. Harper, Elements of Hebrew, (N.Y., Charles Scribner's Sons, 1895)
- Edward Horowitz, How the Hebrew Language Grew (KTAV, 1960)
- Jeff A. Benner, The ancient Hebrew Language and Alphabet (Reading, Pa. Ancient Hebrew Research Center, 00)

Ancient Language and Origins

- Charlton Laird The Miracle of Language (Greenwich Conn., Fawcett, 1953)
- Giorgio Fano, The Origins and Nature of Language, (Bloomington In., Indiana University Press, 1992)
- Jeff A. Benner, The Ancient Hebrew Language and Alphabet (Reading, Pa. Ancient Hebrew Research Center, 00)

Bibles

- Biblia Hebraica Stutgartensia
- The Holy Bible, New International Version (Grand Rapids, Zondervan Bible Publishers, 1973, 1978, 1984)

- The Holy Bible, King James Version

Printed in the United States
134547LV00001B/7/A

9 781589 394575